MW01711803

# Survival Skills for Students

## A Workbook of Learning Strategies

by
James L. Walker, Ph. D.

gage EDUCATIONAL PUBLISHING COMPANY
A DIVISION OF CANADA PUBLISHING CORPORATION
TORONTO ONTARIO CANADA

*Acknowledgments*

Cartoons reprinted with the permission of Sidney Harris, from "CAN'T YOU GUYS READ?" © 1992 , Rutgers University Press.

This publication originated with Manitoba Educational TV and James L. Walker, Ph. D.

ISBN 0-7715-5117-7

Written, printed, and bound in Canada.

1 2 3 4 5 AP 97 96 95 94 93

## CONTENTS

# PREFACE

*Survival Skills for Students : A Workbook of Learning Strategies* was prepared to introduce students to learning strategies to help them do better in school. *Survival Skills for Students* presents a detailed guide to achieving academic success and provides you with a personalized step-by-step guide for learning how to study smarter, not harder.

*Survival Skills for Students* was also designed to address the learning needs of community college, distance education, and correspondence students. Whether you are in college or high school, the learning strategies in *Survival Skills for Students* can help you study more effectively. For most of you, this workbook will be your first introduction to the learning skills which can help you improve your marks, increase your memory, reduce wasted study effort, become more confident about doing well on examinations, and increase your ability to learn.

Every learning strategy included in *Survival Skills for Students* was selected to meet two requirements: (1) the strategy must have a proven effectiveness and (2) it should help students acquire the learning skills which they feel are most important to their own study efforts. Naturally, we wanted to share with you only those learning strategies which have been found to be most effective in helping you become a better student. The strategies you will learn in *Survival Skills for Students* have helped thousands of students like yourself improve their learning skills and achieve higher marks.

The design of this workbook also reflects the priorities and preferences of students like yourself. When we asked large numbers of Manitoba students what strategies would be most helpful and important to them, we found a very strong interest in learning how to get the most out of study time. Most students were not interested in working harder, but they were interested in learning how to work smarter. Students also showed a keen interest in learning how to improve their memory; how to take better notes; how to improve their test-taking skills; and how to increase their reading comprehension. Applying the strategies in *Survival Skills for Students* can help you in each of these areas.

*Survival Skills for Students* is organized in a programmed format. Each learning strategy is preceded by a short self-assessment of your own unique learning needs and interests. Using the results of this assessment, you will be able to move directly to those strategies which are most useful to your own personal learning needs and study priorities. This format allows you to maximize your efforts by concentrating on new learning skills which best fit your own individual needs and desires.

By reading this workbook and applying various learning strategies, you will be taking a major step toward becoming a more successful student. After years of school, some students discover these skills by trial and error, but others often waste hours in inefficient study. *Survival Skills for Students* can help you take the guesswork out of how to get the most out of your study. It can help you master an approach to learning which will not only be reflected in your success in school but will also polish the learning skills so critical to success in most careers.

As you read this workbook, you will see that it reflects my belief that learning should be fun. Please don't let the attempts at humour or the occasional clowning distract or annoy you. Everything in this workbook is presented in the spirit of helping you become a better student.

Please use this workbook in a way which best meets your own learning needs and priorities. Even though you may find that you already know and sometimes use some of the strategies, you may wish to continue reading about them to build your confidence and increase your skill. When you come to strategies which your self-assessment suggests could be useful, devote more attention and practice to them. Learn about these skills, complete the practice activities for them, and start using the new strategies in your studies.

As you learn student survival skills, you will make another important discovery. You will find that you can become a better student. With effort from you and use of this workbook, you will begin a journey of discovery. Your journey will help you become a more successful lifelong learner.

James L. Walker, Ph.D.

# CHAPTER 1
# Getting Started

### In this chapter you can learn

- *how to use this workbook*
- *how to organize for more effective study*
- *how to use goofing off to your advantage*

## How to Use This Workbook

**1**

*Survival Skills for Students* is a programmed book. The contents are arranged in small numbered sections. This programming respects your individuality. It allows you to devote your efforts to those learning strategies which will be most useful to your individual learning style and most helpful in improving your present study habits. The responses you make in each section will direct you to topics and strategies which best fit your own learning needs and preferences.

There is another important reason why the workbook has been programmed. This format respects one of the key principles of how we learn. Although some students think that learning is a passive process where, like a sponge, we "soak" up information, such learning is quite ineffective and is soon forgotten.

Contrary to the old "Passive Theory" of learning, we learn best by actively engaging ourselves during learning. The more active involvement in learning, the better the mastery and retention. Using this principle, the workbook has been designed to engage you in the learning process; to direct you to materials which are most directly relevant to your interests; and to assist your efforts to become more actively involved in learning. As you use the workbook, you'll be asked to make frequent responses, review what you have just learned, and apply newly learned strategies to your academic work. All of these activities will help you master and apply the learning strategies which will make you a better student.

In addition to the programmed sections, you will notice that the workbook contains occasional

"ACTUALLY THIS IS A VERY EXPERIMENTAL COLLEGE. WE HAVE NO CURRICULUM AND NO CLASSES. HOW IT WORKS, ESSENTIALLY, IS IF YOU WANT TO LEARN SOMETHING, YOU GO SOMEPLACE AND YOU LEARN IT."

information boxes. The information presented in these boxes is included at no extra charge and may be read at your leisure. The boxes summarize practical learning tips which may help you fine-tune and further improve your personal learning efficiency. Also included at no extra charge are occasional cartoons which provide comic relief and also illustrate points made in the text.

Let's practise using the programmed features of the workbook by doing a little reflection about your style as a student. Read the following descriptions and check the one that comes closest to describing you.

☐ (a) You are doing poorly in school. Your marks are below average, and you have difficulty getting motivated for school work. You wish you could do better. Extra study doesn't seem to help and you sometimes avoid studying because you find it uninteresting and unproductive in raising your grades.

☞ go to **2**

☐ (b) You are an average student. Your grades contain lots of C's, and perhaps a few B's. You sometimes feel frustrated that even though you spend extra time studying for exams, you usually end up with another C.

☞ go to **3**

☐ (c) You are an above average student. Your grades contain mostly A's and B's. You feel that your learning skills are adequate and you wonder why you're reading this workbook.

☞ go to **4**

☐ (d) You have been away from school for several years and are apprehensive about becoming a student again. You are out of practice at being a student and are worried about making the grade. You don't seem to be able to concentrate as well on your studies as when you were younger and you may be having trouble juggling all of your responsibilities to find time for study.

☞ go to **5**

## 2

If you checked (a), congratulations, you are in the right place! If you checked (b), (c), or (d), you are in the wrong place. Notice the boxed number **2** just above this paragraph, at the left? It indicates that you are now in section **2**. The way to best use this workbook is to follow the directions you are given after you've made a response. Unlike a normal textbook, you should not read this one from cover to cover. Using the programmed instructions will direct your efforts to those sections of most use to you. So, if you checked anything other than (a), please go now to the right section.

Now that we've gotten rid of those students who didn't follow directions (and to think that some of them called themselves good students), a special word to those of you who are doing poorly in school. The fact that you're reading this book suggests that you haven't thrown in the towel or stopped trying. If you are doing poorly in school, the survival skills presented in this workbook can help you develop the learning and study skills to improve your academic performance. You will benefit by paying special attention to the majority of the learning skills included in the workbook. If your school or college has a counsellor who offers help in study skills or a learning assistance centre, you should consider seeking additional help from these sources.

Seeking this extra help is of particular relevance to those of you who may be having problems in school due to difficulties in reading comprehension (a frequent problem among students who are learning English as a second language). Although the learning strategies presented in the workbook can help, if your reading comprehension is poor, you will benefit most from special assistance or courses designed to increase your reading comprehension.

There are dozens of other possible reasons beyond poor reading comprehension which may be causing your poor school performance. It's possible, for example, that you simply are not spending enough time studying. Maybe you find school boring and can't motivate yourself for study. Perhaps you spend plenty of time studying, but haven't learned some basic strategies which can increase your mastery and memory of things studied. If you're like many students who are having difficulty in school, you probably don't have a clear understanding of exactly what is wrong or exactly what you can do to improve your academic performance. This workbook can help. It can help you identify your own learning patterns, eliminate habits or deficiencies which are hurting your grades, and help you develop more effective ways of learning.

☞ go to **6**

## 3

If you checked (b), you've come to the right spot. Like most average students, through trial-and-error, you've probably learned some of the basic learning strategies presented in this workbook. You can use the information presented here to help you sharpen your present skills and to add new skills which will help you become a more successful student. The self-assessments which appear throughout the book will help you pinpoint ways in which your study habits and learning strategies can be improved. Once you've decided that you really want to do better in school, the programmed exercises will help you translate your wishes into reality.

☞ go to **6**

**4**

This is the right section for above average or superior students. Read on. The fact that you are doing well in school probably reflects the general adequacy of your present study skills. Keep up the good work! So, you say, what am I doing reading this book? Even if you are an above average student, there is probably a great deal that you can learn from *Survival Skills for Students* .

A potential danger faced by many above average students is that their presently successful study skills may not adequately serve them when they try new courses, have new instructors, transfer to different schools, or move from high school to college. During my years as an educator, I've seen many above-average students whose marks drastically declined because of one or more of these situations.

Two examples come to mind of above average students who experienced serious academic difficulties because of limited study skills. In one case, a highly successful graduate student in anatomy decided to pursue a degree in biological psychology. Although her skills at mastering and remembering the details of anatomy had served her well, she nearly failed her psychology courses. Only after mastering new learning strategies which allowed her to make the transition from memorization of facts to understanding of concepts and generalizations was she able to improve her grades. In short, the psychology courses required different study skills than those the student had used for her anatomy courses.

The second example of an above average student who found himself in academic hot water because of limited study skills is drawn upon my own experience as a student. In high school, I was an above average student receiving mostly A's and B's. The transition from high school to college nearly ended my academic ambitions. First year university was a disaster! Not only did my A's and B's disappear, but they were replaced by lots of C's, some D's (and yes, even one F). What was wrong? I was working harder than ever yet doing worse than ever. The study skills I acquired during high school were not serving me well in meeting the extra demands and increased competition in my college courses. Unfortunately, no books such as this one or courses in study skills were available at the time. I roughed it out, and laboriously discovered new learning strategies which improved my grades. (Where was this workbook when I needed it?)

The point of this discussion is that even though you are an above average student, you can probably benefit from *Survival Skills for Students*. Give it a shot. I predict that you'll find strategies which can make your study more effective.

☞ go to **6**

**5**

If you checked (d), you're in the right place now. You're an adult returning to academic studies after an absence of several years. The prospect and experience of returning to school can be a profoundly frightening one. If you are like most adult learners, you worry that your learning skills may be rusty; you're apprehensive about competing with younger students; and you wonder how you can possibly juggle all of your responsibilities to find study time.

In fact, the most frequently reported difficulty in returning to school reported by adult learners is insufficient time for their studies. This is understandable when you consider that many adult students are working full-time and trying to balance the roles of spouse, employee, and parent. Finding the time to manage your duties as a student in addition to all of your other responsibilities will be your first important effort as a returning adult student. This situation is especially true of adult students who are studying part-time, taking evening courses, or correspondence courses. If you are in this situation, you will find that the sections of this book which examine strategies for finding time for study and managing your time more efficiently will be of particular value.

In addition to learning new ways to become organized for your role as an adult student, you will also find special learning strategies highlighted throughout the workbook which can help you with academic problems frequently experienced by adult learners. Be sure to pay special attention to these materials.

☞ go to **6**

## 6

Prior sections of this chapter have explained how this book is organized and have given you the chance to examine what type of student you are and how new learning strategies might benefit your own needs. It's time now for our first little quiz.

Based on what you have read so far in this workbook, briefly describe the "passive" theory of learning, and the current view of "active learning."

*the Passive Theory of learning* ____________________

__________________________________________________

__________________________________________________

*the Active Theory of learning* ____________________

__________________________________________________

__________________________________________________

If you have no idea of what we're talking about, return to paragraphs 2 and 3 of Section 1 and re-read this material. After you have read these paragraphs again, return here and try the quiz once more.

If you described the "Passive theory" of learning as the old (and inaccurate) view of learning, you are correct. This notion thinks of learning as a passive process in which we simply "soak up" information. The current and more accurate view of learning reflects the finding that we learn best by being actively involved in the learning process.

As you progress through the rest of this workbook, you will discover that many of the survival strategies are designed to increase your active participation in the learning process. Without trying to steal any thunder from subsequent chapters, let's begin right now and start applying the principle of Active Learning to your progress in this workbook.

One way to become more actively involved in the learning process is to set goals for yourself. If, for example, you approach a reading assignment with certain goals in mind, your motivation and interest will be higher. Concentration will improve as a result, and your retention of the material will be better. It also helps to start a reading assignment with a set of self-generated questions. Then, when you read the materials, you'll be more actively engaged in reading to try to find the answers to your questions. (We'll talk more about this later when we discuss the "SQ3R" strategy for reading textbooks.)

OK, let's start applying these Active Learning strategies right now. If you haven't done so already, return to the front of the workbook and read the Contents page.

The contents page will give you a general idea of the strategies and topics which are covered in the book. You've already done a little reflection on what type of a student you are and what some of your academic and learning needs might be. Using this as a start, spend a few minutes thinking of three specific personal goals which you hope to achieve from reading this book.

**Write down your three learning goals here.**

**1.** ______________________________________________

__________________________________________________

__________________________________________________

**2.** ______________________________________________

__________________________________________________

__________________________________________________

**3.** ______________________________________________

__________________________________________________

__________________________________________________

Now think of some specific questions about what you need to know to reach each of your goals. Try to think of three very specific questions relating to each goal. For example, if one of your specific goals was "to learn how to be less anxious during exams," three specific questions about how to reach this goal might be:
(1) Would I be less anxious if I spaced my study several weeks before the exam rather than trying to cram it all into the last few hours before the test?

(2) How can I study more effectively so I end up being less anxious during exams because I know more?

(3) Are there any special test-taking skills which can improve my exam performance?

Now you try it. Take each of your goals and think of three questions you would like answered about each learning goal.

**Write down your learning questions here.**

**Goal 1**

Question (1) ______________________________________

__________________________________________________

Question (2) ______________________________________

__________________________________________________

Question (3) ______________________________________

__________________________________________________

**Goal 2**

Question (1) ______________________________________

__________________________________________________

Question (2) ______________________________________

__________________________________________________

Question (3) ______________________________________

__________________________________________________

**Goal 3**

Question (1) ______________________________________

__________________________________________________

Question (2) ______________________________________

__________________________________________________

Question (3) ______________________________________

__________________________________________________

Have you written down three personal goals you hope to attain from reading this book? Have you also written down three questions you would like to answer about how to reach each of your learning goals? **If the answer is yes to both questions, go to 7 now**, otherwise continue reading here.

I assume you're still reading here because you didn't complete your goals and questions. If you haven't written down three learning goals and nine learning questions, **go to 8 now.**

## 7

Good! If you're following directions, at this point you have come up with three learning goals and nine learning questions. You've made the first step in applying the important strategy of Active Learning to how much you will learn and remember from reading this workbook.

Why the big deal about setting goals and asking questions before reading a text? Stated simply, setting learning goals and asking learning questions is one important way to become more actively involved in the learning process. Once you have asked some questions, your mind automatically searches for answers as you read. In other words, your reading becomes a more purposeful and involved activity. During reading you will be actively searching for answers. The automatic result of the entire process is that there is a very good likelihood that once you come across the answer to one of your questions, you will remember it better than if you were not actively searching.

We'll have more to say about Active Learning later. For now, you're off to a good start. As you work through the sections of the workbook, keep an eye out for information which is related to your goals and which answers the questions you have posed.

☞ **go to 9**

## 8

If you are reading this section, it should be because you didn't write down three learning goals and nine learning questions. As the old board game says "Go directly to jail, do not pass go, do not collect $200."

Old habits die hard. You may be so used to reading a text straight through from start to finish that you continued with this pattern rather than pausing to come up with your goals and questions. Maybe it just seemed like too much trouble to stop, think, and write. Perhaps you didn't have a pencil or pen handy. Whatever the reason, your first step in applying the strategy of Active Learning to improving your own study effectiveness is to start practicing this skill. You're short changing yourself if you don't give it a try! With this little "pep talk" in hand (along with a pen or pencil in the other hand), **go back to 6** and write down your goals and questions.

9

## Organizing for More Efficient Study

This part of the chapter shares survival strategies to help you become more organized for study. All of the strategies have been shown to be helpful in improving study efficiency. You may be already using some of these strategies. If so, congratulations, you've discovered for yourself some of the study secrets of master students. To help you decide if each strategy would be useful in your own case, each section starts with a short quiz about your present learning habits. The results of your quiz will point you to sections which are likely to be most useful to you.

When using the self-quiz to evaluate your study habits, be honest with yourself. Fill out the quiz to show your usual study habits, and use the results to move to those sections which might help you improve or polish your present study habits.

| Yes | No | |
|---|---|---|
| ☐ | ☐ | 1. Do you usually study in the same place? |
| ☐ | ☐ | 2. Is your study place quiet and free of distractions? |
| ☐ | ☐ | 3. Do you usually have few interruptions during your study? |

If you answered "Yes" to each of these items, the chances are good that you have learned the importance of studying in the same regular place; that you have a study place which is quiet and free of distractions; and that you try to arrange your studying so that you will have few interruptions. Keep up the good work! These strategies are the basic student survival skills you will need for more effective and efficient studying. Please go to 11 now.

Continue reading here if you answered "No" to any of the items.

If you answered "No" to one or more of the three questions, you can benefit by learning how to make a few simple changes in the place you select for most of your regular study, and by learning some new ways of reducing the interruptions which interfere with your concentration during study. Go to 10 .

10

## The "Three P's" of Organizing for More Efficient Study: Place, Preparation, and Posture

**Where do you study?** The best strategy is to find a quiet room where people will leave you alone. If possible, find one regular study place and do the bulk of your studying there. Do nothing there except study. This will help your mind associate this place with study. After you develop this habit, every time you sit down at your study spot, you will automatically have a strong "mental set" for studying.

Of course, a good regular study spot should be well-lighted (to reduce strain on your eyes), and should be comfortable (but not so comfortable that you'll fall asleep!).

### Reducing Distractions in Your Study Place

If your regular study place is in your home, ask the other members of your family not to interrupt you when you are in your study spot. Try to select a study place away from other household activities. An ideal place is a room where you can be by yourself and close the door.

One of the major reasons for inefficient study time is the tendency for many of us to become distracted during our studies. By engineering the right study conditions, you can automatically help to increase your learning efficiency. Here are some strategies which can help. Review them, and apply those which seem most relevant to your own situation.

❏ Ask others not to interrupt you during study unless the house is burning down, you have just won the lottery, or something else of equal earth-shaking magnitude has occurred.

❏ Minimize other distractions during study. It's probably not a good idea to study with the television on. Your attention will automatically be distracted by the TV.

❏ Do you study while listening to music? Some students find that soft instrumental background music helps mask other more distracting noises. In fact there is research evidence that certain kinds of music (very slow tempo baroque music such as Bach and Vivaldi) may actually improve memory. Unfortunately, few of you probably naturally favour baroque music and you may play your chosen music so loud that it distracts from your concentration. Try this simple test the next time you study with music. Every time you find yourself actually listening to the music, make a mark on a piece of paper. If you have more than a few marks on the paper at the end of your study session, the music is probably more of a distraction than a help to your studies.

❏ If background music is loud or contains lyrics, it will almost always distract you from your studies. Your attention is automatically directed toward any loud sound. You also automatically focus your attention on any sound containing words. Don't fool yourself. Even though that rock music might be pretty pleasing to your ears, your brain will automatically focus on understanding the words. Part of your attention will switch to the music at the expense of your reading. Increase your efficiency by turning off music or TV while you study. You'll finish sooner and then you can watch TV or listen to music when you can really enjoy it.

❏ If someone telephones during a study time, ask a member of your family to take a message. Call them back later during a study break.

❏ Keep your study area reasonably organized and neat. You don't have to be a neatness freak, but if your study area is a mess, you may tend to avoid it. A desktop cluttered with papers can also be distracting. While you're reading that Biology text, you'll notice that pile of letters or bills out of the corner of your eye and you'll find yourself thinking about them rather than your textbook. Keep your desk clear of everything except for current reading and work materials.

❏ When you must study away from your regular study spot, try to pick a place with few distractions. Unless you have superhuman powers of concentration, it's probably not a good idea to spend much time trying to study in a student canteen or cafeteria. These spots are usually a beehive of distractions. Spend time here if you want to eat, socialize, or relax, but don't expect to get much high quality work done in these environments. A secluded study desk in your school library will be much more likely to produce high quality study results.

❏ Use the washroom before you start studying.

These strategies can automatically assist your efforts to "study smarter, not harder." Take a few moments now to reflect on your own study situation. What positive changes could you make to where you study and how you manage distractions? Develop your own personal plan by completing this short exercise.

*I plan to increase my study efficiency by making the following changes in where I study and how I manage distractions:*

---------------------------------------------
---------------------------------------------
---------------------------------------------
---------------------------------------------
---------------------------------------------
---------------------------------------------
---------------------------------------------
---------------------------------------------
---------------------------------------------
---------------------------------------------
---------------------------------------------
---------------------------------------------
---------------------------------------------

☞ go to **11**

**11**

**Preparation for Study** Getting organized for more efficient study involves preparation. Use this checklist to see if your preparation needs polish.

| Yes | No | |
|---|---|---|
| ❑ | ❑ | 1. I know when my "best study times" are and I schedule study time accordingly. |
| ❑ | ❑ | 2. I "psych myself up" before I sit down to study. |
| ❑ | ❑ | 3. When I sit down to study, every thing I need (pen, pencils, paper, texts, etc.) is usually right at hand. |
| ❑ | ❑ | 4. I'm usually careful to take care of my physical needs (bathroom, eating, nap, etc) before I start studying. |

If you can honestly answer "Yes" to each of these items, you are probably doing a pretty efficient job of organizing your study preparation. Feel free to read the rest of this section if you're interested, otherwise, go to **12**.

If you're still reading here, it should be because you answered "No" to some of the items in the study quiz, or are especially interested in polishing your existing study skills. In this section we'll review four preparation strategies which can help set the stage for more successful study.

**Using your best times to advantage** Most of us have times during the day when our energy level is highest and when we do our best work. Are you a morning person who works best early in the day? If so, try to squeeze in some quality study time early in the day.

Are you the type of person who comes alive only after sunset? In this case you may want to schedule some study time during those evening hours when you feel most alert.

Maybe mid-afternoon is the time of day when you feel at your best. If so, reserve some of these hours for study.

The trick to using your peak times to your best advantage is to schedule study for these times and to use other times for other activities which don't require as much mental effort and concentration. Start by reflecting on your own daily ups-and-downs. Notice those times when you are at your mental best and also those times during which thinking seems to be a chore. Once you have discovered your personal pattern, apply this information to increasing your study efficiency by reserving some peak times for study and learning.

Let me illustrate by describing how I apply this strategy to my own work. I'm a morning person. I'm at my mental best in the morning hours and I have another smaller burst of peak time in the early evening. My worst times are for about an hour after lunch and again right after dinner. So how do I apply this knowledge to my work habits? First, when possible, I try to reserve some morning hours for work which is difficult or requires a high degree of concentration or creativity. Less demanding work is allocated to afternoon hours. The hours after eating when I'm at my lowest are reserved for activities other than work or other undemanding chores. If necessary, I know that I've got another evening "window of opportunity" when I'm capable of doing some pretty efficient work.

You can use the same principle within an individual study session. Let's say that you have allocated two hours for study. Chances are you'll be at your best during the first part of this study session. During the second hour you're more likely to be getting tired and perhaps a little restless. Your study will probably be more effective if you spend the first (rather than the second) hour on coursework which you find more difficult or challenging. Then use the final hour for courses which you find easier or less demanding.

**"Psych" Yourself Up for Study** Although some psychologists might cringe at the phrase "psyching yourself up for study," they wouldn't argue with the idea that going into an activity with the proper mental set will increase the efficiency with which you perform the activity. Study is no exception. If you begin study with the wrong mental set, your motivation, interest, and concentration can all go "down the tubes."

Imagine how much fun studying will be if you are saying to yourself beforehand "Oh great! Another hour wrestling with those ridiculous math problems." Instead, suppose that prior to starting your math assignments you say to yourself "You know, I do feel pretty good about it whenever I figure out how to solve one of those problems. I'm going to give it a good shot during the next hour." This mental set will start you off with the right positive thinking to stimulate a more productive study session.

Try "psyching yourself up for study" the next time you prepare for study. You'll be surprised at the power of this simple strategy of positive thinking!

**Have Your Study Materials Handy** Like a dog-catcher without a net, your job as a student will be more difficult if you don't have your materials handy. The shelves and drawers of your regular study spot should be well stocked with the tools of the student's trade. In addition to textbooks and class notes, your "tools" should include paper, writing instruments, a dictionary and perhaps a thesaurus, folders or binders for organizing your notes, an assignment diary, and a study schedule (more on this later).

Depending on what courses you are taking, other materials (calculator, compass, drawing pens, drafting instruments, typewriter, etc.) might also be helpful and these too should be ready and handy when you need them.

If you spend time during the day studying away from your usual study place, make sure you bring the materials you'll need with you for the day. It's going to be more difficult using that mid-day hour at the library to finish your math assignment when you discover (horror of horrors!) that you've forgotten your calculator.

**Take Care of Your Body First** Take care of your bodily needs first. It's hard to concentrate if you're hungry, have to go to the bathroom, are tired, or are feeling stiff from sitting down all day long. Perhaps a short nap will leave you fresher and with better concentration (a good night's sleep will help even more.) Rather than thinking about food every 20 seconds when you are trying to study, maybe you would be better off if you ate a little something before studying. If your muscles are rebelling from forced inactivity, give them a break with a little exercise. Either precede your study time with some physical exercise or do something physical during one of your study breaks. (See later sections for more on the benefits of "goofing off.")

☞ **go to 14**

**12**

**Finding the Best Position for Study** Complete this quiz to see if you should read this section.

| Yes | No | |
|---|---|---|
| ❑ | ❑ | 1. I often feel sleepy or drowsy during study. |
| ❑ | ❑ | 2. I spend a lot of time during study changing positions and fidgeting. |
| ❑ | ❑ | 3. My muscles or back gets stiff and a little sore during study. |

If you answered "No" to each of the above items, you probably don't have any problems with your posture or position during study. Go to **13**.

If you answered "Yes" to any of these items, your posture during study may be causing you some difficulties. Continue reading this section to see if you could make a few simple changes which might improve your ability to get the most out of your study time.

Considerable difference of opinion exists between students versus parents and teachers concerning the "best" studying position. Is it best, for example, to sit at a desk or can you study as well comfortably settled back in a favourite easy chair?

Although most good students report that they choose to sit at a desk during study, other students feel that they are equally alert when lying on a bed, sitting in an easy chair, or lying on the floor. Your posture may be robbing you of effective study time if you find that you become sleepy after a few minutes of study, spend a lot of time fidgeting and changing your position during study, or feel muscular soreness.

Keep an eye out for these symptoms. If you have them, consider changing your posture or position during study. In my own case, I've learned that 15 minutes after settling into an easy chair the force of gravity on my eyelids becomes overwhelming. The problem is, of course, easily eliminated by doing serious reading and study while at my desk.

Although posture can play a role in causing fatigue and sleepiness during study, it's not the only possible cause. Other factors to consider include poor lighting, eye problems, general lack of sleep, poor nutrition, and low motivation. If you're chronically tired during study, make sure your work area is well illuminated, have your eyes examined, and try to make sure you are getting the six to eight hours of sleep every day that most of us need if we are to function at our best. Muscular strain, if present, might be corrected by taking more frequent short exercise and stretch breaks or by experimenting with different chairs or the height of your chair.

**13**

## How to Goof Off To Advantage

Since most students have at some time probably longed to hear something good said about goofing off, we now offer you this "once in a lifetime opportunity." Read carefully so you can learn all about the benefits of goofing off!

Goofing off should probably be an important part of every study plan. In fact, as you develop your own study schedule (more on this in a later chapter), it's wise to include a number of short goofing-off breaks into every study session.

Sorry to disappoint you, but notice that the word "short" was stressed. If your study sessions contain 90% goofing-off breaks and 10% study, you should probably go back to the drawing board. On the other hand, if your study sessions contain 90% study and 10% goofing off, you are probably close to achieving an ideal balance for the benefits of constructive goofing off.

Short study breaks (also known as goofing off) can be a big help to your concentration. If you have things other than your studies which you are thinking about, you'll know that you can think about these things during an upcoming study break.

To get the most out of a planned study break, you should probably get up, move around, and for a short time do something entirely different. Have a snack, walk around, talk with someone, do something to get your blood moving again.

During study, our minds can work at top efficiency for only a limited time. A study break, taken when you notice that you've been staring at the same page for 15 minutes, can leave you feeling more alert when you return to your studies.

Although study breaks are essential to a good study plan, some students end up using them as excuses for not studying. Some study skills experts suggest that a good balance of study and break times for high school students is 45 minutes of study followed by a ten minute break. College students may be able to study efficiently for somewhat longer periods without a break.

To get the most out of your own study and break routine, watch your own reactions during study. For example, if your attention and concentration generally flag after about 30 minutes, maybe this is the best time to work in a ten minute study break. As you work through this book and learn to increase your concentration span, you'll be able to gradually lengthen periods of good concentration before you need to take a break.

One last word about the goofing-off break. Many top students use their study breaks as rewards for periods of effective study. They make an unwritten contract with themselves that after so many minutes of work, they'll use their break as a little reward for their work. This little trick can help you feel good about reaching your study goal and at the same time help increase your motivation for study. Give it a try.

☞ go to **15**

**14**

It's review time! Without looking back, see how many of the main points about preparing for study you remember from section **11** .

Answer the following review questions.

**List and briefly describe the four strategies of maximizing how you prepare for study.**

Strategy 1: ______________________________

______________________________

Basic idea: ______________________________

______________________________

______________________________

______________________________

______________________________

______________________________

Strategy 2: ______________________________

______________________________

Basic idea: ______________________________

______________________________

______________________________

______________________________

______________________________

______________________________

Strategy 3: ______________________________

______________________________

Basic idea: ______________________________

______________________________

______________________________

______________________________

______________________________

______________________________

Strategy 4: ______________________________

______________________________

Basic idea: ______________________________

______________________________

______________________________

______________________________

______________________________

______________________________

☞ **go to 16**

**15**

Congratulations! You've made it to the end of Chapter 1. At this point in your journey toward becoming a more effective learner you've had a chance to examine many of your present study skills. You've learned that the best way to read a text is not always straight through from the first page to the last. Maybe you've picked up some ideas about how you can get organized for more effective study. (The really neat thing about most of these strategies is that they work and they don't require much work from you!)

During your travels through Chapter 1 you also may have picked up some ideas about little tricks to help reduce the number of interruptions during study times. (Forgotten them already? If so, go back to section **10** for a quick review.)

Speaking of review, notice how we've included several review exercises in Chapter 1? We've done this to start getting you into the habit of making quick reviews after you've read something. It's one of the guaranteed ways of helping you remember what you've read and it's a survival strategy we'll be telling you more about in later chapters.

Lastly, Chapter 1 shared some light-hearted ways of using goofing off to help you become a more effective learner. You learned of the necessity for building breaks into your study schedule, why these breaks are essential to maintaining good concentration, and how you can use these breaks to reward yourself for meeting your study goals.

As you've seen, this is a programmed book. You read only those sections which seem most directly related to your own needs and interests. Each chapter can be read independently and in any order. Alternatively, the book can be read in the order in which the chapters are presented.You can best decide how to use the workbook. Take a minute now to review the learning goals you selected in section **6**. Then choose one approach:

- ☐ Go to the contents page and select your greatest problem area. Then go to the chapter which deals with it most directly. Or,
- ☐ Go to Chapter 2 and start working through the workbook in the order in which the chapters are presented.

**Before reading more, take a goofing-off break!**

**16**

Your answers to the questions in section **10** should look something like this:

Strategy 1: *Use my peak times to study more effectively.*
Basic idea: *Identify times during the day when I'm generally at my best and reserve some of these times for study. Use my peak times for coursework which I find difficult or challenging. Reserve other times for more routine and less demanding tasks.*

Strategy 2: *"Psych" Myself Up for Study.*
Basic Idea: *Developing a positive mental set before studying can help make my study more effective by increasing my motivation and concentration.*

Strategy 3: *Keep my study materials organized and at hand.*
Basic Idea: *Keeping all of the study materials handy where I'll need them will help prevent interruptions during study to fetch things I need.*

Strategy 4: *Look after my bodily needs before starting a study session.*
Basic Idea: *The needs of my body should come first. My study time will be less effective if I'm hungry, or tired.*

If you couldn't remember the main ideas, or if your answers were quite different from these, go back to section **11**. Reread the section and try again.

If your answers were similar to these, give yourself a big smile for spotting and remembering the main ideas. Now go back to **12**.

# CHAPTER 2
# Motivation and Concentration

**In this chapter you can learn**

- *how to become more motivated for study*
- *how to become more interested in your coursework*
- *how to increase your powers of concentration*

This chapter contains survival strategies to help you become more motivated for learning, develop a greater interest in your studies, and increase your concentration abilities. Studies of outstanding students have found that they tend to share something in common. They are usually well motivated for study. They are interested and sometimes even enthusiastic about their studies. They also have developed the ability to focus and maintain attention and concentration during study.

These traits serve a student well. They make study more interesting, enjoyable, and efficient. Study isn't nearly the chore when you've got the motivation and interest, and you'll get more out of study time as you improve your powers of concentration.

How do you stack up as a student? Is there room to fine-tune your motivations for doing well in coursework, your interest in courses and how well you concentrate during study? Take this little self-quiz to see if the sections on motivation will be useful to you.

| Yes | No | |
|---|---|---|
| ☐ | ☐ | 1. I enjoy most of my courses because of the interesting information they contain. |
| ☐ | ☐ | 2. I am usually highly motivated to do well in my courses. |
| ☐ | ☐ | 3. Sometimes, study is actually fun (or at least enjoyable). |
| ☐ | ☐ | 4. None of my courses are boring to me. (Mark "Yes" if this applies to you, mark "No" if some of your courses are boring.) |
| ☐ | ☐ | 5. I have specific life or career goals which my courses will help me reach. |
| ☐ | ☐ | 6. Getting motivated to study is not usually a problem for me. (Mark "Yes" if this applies to you, mark "No" if you sometimes have trouble getting motivated to study.) |
| ☐ | ☐ | 7. In every course I'm taking, I can usually find something of interest . |
| ☐ | ☐ | 8. When I'm in a motivational slump, I give myself "motivational pep talks" to get moving again on my studies. |
| ☐ | ☐ | 9. A low mark on an examination never stops me from continuing to do my best in the course. (Mark "Yes" if you agree, mark"No" if low marks cause you to work less in that course.) |

If you marked "Yes" to each of these items, you are either being less than honest with yourself or you are a "super student." Assuming that you were being honest, you are probably bursting at the seams with energy and excitement for your academic pursuits. Any more motivation and you'd probably explode. Of course we wouldn't want this to happen, so you had better skip the sections on motivation.

☞ go to **2**

If you answered "No" to some of the above items, please **go to** **1**.

**1**

If you're reading here, you may be poorly motivated for study, or just interested in learning how to become better motivated for school work. Like most students, you may do better in courses which match your interests and wish you were as interested in all your courses. This section can give you some hints about how to become a more motivated student.

**Motivation and Study** Lack of motivation for study has probably caused more failures and lowered more grades than lack of ability.

Without motivation, study becomes a chore. Forcing yourself to sit down and study, you spend the time wishing you were doing something else. Effective study under these conditions is difficult.

The best and most powerful motivation comes from inside. It is self generated. Others can help you trigger this type of motivation (a good teacher, for example), but the motivation itself is ultimately from within yourself. You are motivated to work to achieve your needs and goals. Motivation runs low when you don't see the work leading to something you want.

Some motivation comes naturally. You're motivated to eat when hungry. You're motivated to work when you need money. You're motivated to get in shape before a big track meet. And, if you're like most students, you're motivated to study subjects that you find naturally interesting. Unfortunately, many of your courses may not fall in this category. How do you motivate yourself for courses you don't find naturally interesting? Worse yet, how can you whip up a little interest in courses you may find downright boring?

One of the first steps in trying to increase your motivation for study is to do some self-reflection about the sorts of things that are important to you. Think about the goals you value. It may help to see how many other students feel about these things. Have a look at Box 1 (on this page) which summarizes some of the goals which motivate other students like yourself.

Because you are the final author of your own goals, you can control your motivation for study.

**Continue on to section 2** to see how to use personal goals to enhance your motivation for study.

Box 1

### What Motivates Other Students?

Like anyone, students are motivated by a variety of goals and aspirations. Some motives are stronger, others weaker, and certain individuals may not have any of the following motives. Read about each of these student motives and ask yourself how you compare.

**Interest** Some students are motivated by a strong natural interest or curiosity (at least for some of their courses). Because they are curious or interested in a subject, they want to know more about it. Their studies help them reach this goal. When possible, students choose courses which match their interests. College students generally have more choice of courses than do high school students, although some elective courses are possible at the high school level.

**Ambition** Some students are motivated by ambition. They have a strong desire to do well in whatever they try. It's important for them to succeed. These students often see doing well in their courses as the first step in reaching a point in their life where they are earning enough to have a comfortable standard of living.

**Responsibility** Most students are also somewhat motivated by a sense of responsibility. They want to do well in their school work because it is expected of them and will please their parents. Students who are married and have their own families may feel the responsibility of doing well in school work so they can increase their earning potential and better support their family. Like natural interest and ambition, a sense of responsibility can be a powerful motive for study.

**Competition** Some students thrive on competition. The desire to be among the best can be a powerful driving force for them. They bring the same spirit of dedication and effort to their studies that Olympic hopefuls show in training.

**Perfectionism** A few students are motivated by the desire to reach excellence in everything they do. They're not happy with anything less than perfection and they can may drive themselves very hard trying to reach a self-imposed standard of excellence.

**Challenge** Other students are motivated by the challenge of school work. Like a mountain climber, they do it simply because "it's there." The more difficult the course, the more this sense of challenge is aroused. Sometimes the motive can actually backfire and these students do poorly in courses they perceive as easy.

**Personal Growth** Although they may not think about it in exactly these terms, some students are motivated by the desire to grow and develop as a person. They want to learn more about the world, become a more learned and educated person, and acquire new skills.

*Just imagine the great job you could do as a student if you had all of these motivations for your coursework!*

(As a point of interest, this is a good spot to share the findings of a recently conducted study of goals and values of some university students. The students ranked these goals as most important: Being well off financially; helping others in difficulty; becoming an authority in their field; raising a family; getting married; obtaining recognition from colleagues; developing a meaningful philosophy of life; influencing social values; helping promote racial understanding; and having administrative responsibility.)

☞ go to 2

**2**

**Putting Goals to Work for You** Studies of above-average students have found that most of them have given some thought to their short-term and long-term goals. These students use goals to help give them an important sense of direction. Almost always, good students include getting good grades as one of their most important short-term goals. Getting a degree, a good job, or going on for advanced education or training is a frequent long-term goal for the best students.

When students have difficulty getting motivated to study, it may be due to a lack of goals. Have you thought about your own short-term and long-term goals? Have you thought about how your school work will help you reach these goals? Spend a few minutes now thinking about what is important to you. What would you like to be? How will you reach your goals?

Remember how you used to diagram sentences in language arts class? Diagramming was designed to help you identify the major parts of a sentence and see how the parts are related to each other. You can do the same thing with your goals. A "Goal Diagram" will help you identify your goals and see how they are related to each other. Let's look at the "Goal Diagram" of one student as an example.

Joe is starting his final year of high school. He would like to become a computer programmer. He likes his math classes, but has little interest in other courses. Joe's Goal Diagram looks like this:

### *Joe's Goal Diagram*

**Long-Term Goals**

1. Graduate from high school with an above-average grade record.
2. Become a computer programmer.
3. Get a good job as a computer programmer.
4. Get married and raise a family.

**Short-Term Goals**

1. Receive a B (or better) in my courses this term.
2. Receive an A in my math and computer science courses.
3. Review the first four chapters of history before the test.
4. Copy the physics notes for the day I was absent.

**Near-Term Goals**

1. Complete all math problems by Wednesday.
2. Get physics notes from Melissa.
3. Read at least 20 pages of the history text.
4. Review course notes from past weeks.
5. Ask Melissa to go to the movies on Saturday night.

Joe's Goal Diagram identifies some of his major long-term goals and highlights some short-term or intermediate goals which will help him reach his longer-term goals. His near-term goals are things he will do in the next few days to help him attain goals higher in his goal diagram. These are related to the longer term, larger goals.

Don't be discouraged if you don't have any longer-term goals. It's quite common for young people not to know exactly what job or career they want. Even if you don't yet have a career in mind, it's good to get used to the idea of thinking about your future.

The thing to keep in mind about a Goal Diagram is that working to achieve your short-term goals will allow you the freedom to choose what you want to do with your life. Your short-term goals are the foundation upon which the rest of your goals will stand or fall.

☞ go to **4**

**3**

Good students use a variety of different strategies to maintain their motivation. After all, those long-term goals are a long way off. Sometimes it seems that they're so far away that you can't see much connection with what you're doing right now and that distant goal. If you are interested in additional strategies used by good students to motivate themselves, read Box 2.

**Fifteen Tips for Increasing Your Motivation**

Setting personal goals and working to reach these goals is the first step to increasing your motivation for schoolwork. What then? The following strategies have been used by many students like yourself to become more motivated for their studies.

Discover and apply those strategies you think will be most useful for **you**.

- Take a course for which you are poorly motivated and work it into your "Goal Diagram." Think how doing well in that course will fit into your longer term goals. (For example, that course in Language Arts you find so boring might fit into your goals more closely than you think. Will effort aimed at improving your written communication skills help land a better job? In most cases, the answer would be "Yes".)

- Put your Goal Diagram in a place where you can look at it before studying. Reread it occasionally to remind you of your reasons for studying.

- Check off the near-term and short-term goals as you achieve them. Feel good about your achievements. Give yourself a reward for reaching goals. As you complete goals, add new ones.

- Try competing with yourself. See if you can do better on the next test. Can you write a better paper next time? Can you raise your present marks by a full letter grade? Can you find something in your most boring course that interests you and will be useful in improving your skills and knowledge?

- Does everyone (including yourself) think of you as a poor student? Get down to work and prove them wrong!

- Try making a contract with yourself. Your contract should outline your goals for each course and the reward you'll give yourself for reaching those goals.

- Make sure that you set small enough near-term goals so that they can be realistically reached. Big goals may seem so remote or so difficult that you are overwhelmed into inactivity whenever you think about them.

- Think about where you want to be in five years. Do you visualize yourself working in a boring job at minimum wage? Or do you see yourself in a career which matches your interests and has a real future? What you do right now in your schoolwork will influence that future.

- Stop blaming others for your poor school performance. When you find that you are doing poorly, face the situation honestly. Remind yourself that you may not be taking your schoolwork seriously enough. Work on your motivation. Remember that you alone are responsible for your own failure or success. Use this motivational "pep talk" to create the motivation to dig in and get to work. Don't let yourself down.

- Feel good about what you know and what you are learning. Take a real pleasure in learning something new. Use newly acquired knowledge in your thinking. Share it with friends.

- Remind yourself that anything really worthwhile requires hard work to achieve. Mastering your coursework is no exception. Feel good about your hard work.

- Stop making excuses for why you are not motivated. Refuse to accept "it's too boring" as an excuse for not studying. Read the sections in this chapter on how to make your studies more interesting.

- Don't let a subject you find difficult get you down. Try thinking of it as a "challenge" rather than a "problem."

- When reading a chapter in a textbook, place a book mark at the end of that chapter. This helps set a clear limit to what you have to study during a session, and you can easily observe your progress toward the marker.

- Start and finish your study sessions with your most interesting subjects. Your tendency to avoid studying will be reduced if you know you are going to start on something already interesting to you. Once you're in the swing of working, it'll be easier to continue with less interesting assignments. Try to finish a study session working on a high interest subject. This will help you leave the session feeling more satisfied with what you have done.

☞ go to **5**

**4**

Start fine-tuning your motivation by completing your own "Goal Diagram." Think of three or four long term goals, then list some short-term and near-term goals which will help you reach your longer range objectives.

**Long Term Goals**

1.

2.

3.

4.

**Short-Term Goals**

1.

2.

3.

4.

**Near-Term Goals**

1.

2.

3.

4.

5.

Since this section is about using goals to increase your motivation for study, I hope you've included some school-related goals in your goal diagram. If not, maybe you should revise your diagram and work some more on how your school work fits into your longer range plans.

Once you've completed your goal diagram, you have a "motivational master plan." It points out where you'd like to go and how you'll get there. Your master plan is a valuable way to create and maintain the energy and effort you'll need to devote to your studies. The next time you're putting off study because you're not motivated, recall your master plan. Knowing where you want to go and what you have to do to get there will help create the energy and motivation to get you going.

☞ **go to 3**

**5**

☐ Are you a high school student? If so, go to **6**.

☐ Are you a college student or an adult returning to school? If so, continue reading this section.

High school students typically have few course electives. The courses they take may not be an ideal match for their own special interests even though they meet the goal of providing a sound basic education. As an adult returning to school or as a college student, you typically have more choice in selecting courses specifically related to your major interests or career training needs.

In spite of this, if you find that you have little interest in your courses or are unmotivated to study them, perhaps you should examine your present career or training goals. The counselling service at your college makes its living helping students like yourself make career and course selections which best reflect individual needs, values, interests, and abilities. It's possible that your low motivation results from a mismatch between you and your courses. Check it out by making an appointment with a career counselling professional at your college.

☞ **go to 6**

**6**

## Becoming More Interested in Your Studies

The following sections deal with ways you can become more interested in your studies. Answer the following questions to see if you could benefit from these strategies.

| Yes | No | |
|---|---|---|
| ❑ | ❑ | 1. I sometimes have a hard time maintaining interest in my studies. |
| ❑ | ❑ | 2. I agree with the statement "School is a drag." |
| ❑ | ❑ | 3. Most of my subjects don't seem to have any relationship to my career or job plans. |
| ❑ | ❑ | 4. Doing school work comes in dead last on the list of things I'd like to do. |
| ❑ | ❑ | 5. I can usually whip up some interest in schoolwork, but I'd like to learn more about becoming interested in my courses. |
| ❑ | ❑ | 6. Studying is about as interesting as watching paint dry. |

If you answered "No" to each of these items, please go to **8**.

If you answered "Yes" to one or more of the items, please go to **7**.

**7**

Motivation and interest are closely related. Generally, if you are motivated, you will also be interested. Enthusiastic ski buffs, for example, are usually highly interested in talking about skiing, in visiting sporting goods stores to look at ski equipment, and in reading about skiing.

Which comes first, the motivation or the interest? It's a little like the question about the chicken and the egg. If you are interested in a subject, you will be motivated to pursue that subject. If you are motivated about a subject, you will be naturally interested. The two go hand in hand. Prior sections of this chapter have examined ways to increase your motivation for study. If you are successful in increasing your motivation, you will naturally become more interested in your studies.

The present section attacks the problem from the opposite direction. If you can devise ways to become more interested in your studies, your motivation for study will also naturally increase.

Let's begin by looking at three strategies for increasing interest which have been most successful for other students.

**Strategy 1: Positive Self-Talk**
During waking hours you constantly "talk to yourself." You may ordinarily call it "thinking," but this self-talk is constantly running through your mind. Your self-talk can influence how you feel, what you do, and how you perceive the world. So, how can you use positive self-talk to become more interested in studying?

Let's say that before your usual study time you find yourself thinking something like this: "I sure wish I didn't have all this schoolwork to do tonight. Wouldn't you know it, I'm going to have to miss my favourite TV show. Some people have all the luck,"... etc. etc. You guessed it, this is not an example of positive self-talk.

Negative self-talk such as this sets the stage to find study uninteresting and boring. When you expect something to be boring, it often turns out that way. Your mind automatically looks for aspects of the activity which match your expectations and a self-fulfilling prophecy is born! Worse yet, the negative self-talk may prevent you from ever getting started with your study.

Developing the habit of positive self-talk about your studies can be a powerful strategy in creating the self-fulfilling prophecy that your study time will be interesting and profitable.

**Try practising this strategy yourself.** Before a scheduled study session, try telling yourself positive things about your upcoming learning session. Imagine how good it will feel to have that essay completed before the deadline. Think about the satisfaction you'll feel in learning how to master those new math problems. Remind yourself about how your grades will benefit from your current work. Visualize how your study sessions will gradually lead you toward your career objectives.

Once you develop this type of positive self-talk about your course work, both interest and motivation benefit. You become more interested in your work because you are mentally focusing on benefits rather than negatives. Your interest increases because you have created a clear mental picture of how your present work fits into your master plans. As you practice this positive self-talk strategy, you'll notice that it soon becomes a habit. Give it a try!

**Strategy 2: Become More Actively Involved**
Many students successfully cultivate interest in their studies by increasing their active involvement during study. (As we'll see later, this strategy also increases the amount you learn and remember.) Spend your study time doing something more than just reading. Do more than is expected of you.

Review to yourself what you have just studied or find a study partner and spend some time talking together about ideas or concepts in your coursework. When you run across something you find especially interesting, seek out additional information on that topic. Visit your library and seek more information on the material. Consider looking up a study topic in an encyclopedia and reading more about it. Try looking at some weekly magazines and see how they offer a different approach to the subjects you are currently learning.

Another way of becoming more actively involved in your studies is to always try to relate new information to what you already know. In physics, for example, when you are learning about the principles of leverage, think about the last time you tried to lift something really heavy. How could what you have just learned about levers have made the job easier? Or think about how your family wheelbarrow is a good example of a "2nd class lever" in which the load is balanced between the fulcrum and the effort. The point, of course, is to make that little bit of extra effort to see the relevance of what you've just learned to what you already know. It's a great way to help you become more interested in your studies!

**Strategy 3: Develop Your Sense of Curiosity**
Curiosity may have "killed the cat," but it's the lifeblood of interest in your studies. Like most traits, we can train ourselves to show more curiosity. Before and during your studies, why not try to see if you can generate some curiosity about the material you are studying. Ask yourself questions about what you'll be reading (this also helps you remember what you've read).

Develop the habit of asking yourself questions that begin with these phrases: "I wonder why...?"; "What would happen if...?"; "How is this related to...?"; "What is important about...?"; and "How can I apply this to my own life?" If you start a study session with these questions in mind, you have an extra reason for studying. You'll be reading to satisfy your own curiosity!

As an example of how you might approach increasing your interest through curiosity, let's consider how this strategy might be applied to a chemistry course. My own student career as a chemist was short lived. Somehow, I just couldn't see much in chemistry except a mass of information and equations which I would have to memorize. Even after a full year of chemistry in college, my interest in the subject was at the bottom of the scale (along with my marks).

Unfortunately, as a student I never reached the point where I tried to create some personal interest in the subject. I have no doubt that my interest in chemistry could have been vastly increased if I had known enough to try to become more curious. There were dozens of questions I might have become curious about. Why does iron rust? Why does coal burn? Why do the leaves change colour in the fall? What happens in a battery that produces electricity? How does lightning change the air and help fertilize plants? Will it ever be possible to change iron into gold? You get the idea. There are thousands of interesting questions you could be asking yourself about the subject of chemistry or any other course.

Asking yourself these questions will be a powerful help in becoming more interested in the subject. In fact, becoming more curious wins on nearly every count. Asking yourself questions not only stimulates your interest and helps you become an active learner, it also gives you a rewarding feeling of accomplishment when you discover answers. Become more interested in your studies by becoming more curious.

☞ go to **10**

**8**

One of the reasons you're probably reading this workbook is to learn ways to "study smarter" without "studying harder." I'm not suggesting that study and learning isn't hard work. Efforts to discover ways to learn without any work (such as "sleep learning") have been remarkably unsuccessful. In fact, we now know that the most efficient learning and memory result from Active Learning. As discussed before, this type of learning requires active participation in the learning process. So, isn't there some way to get more out of your work so that you can be working smarter, not harder?

Don't despair, the answer is "Yes." Most students can profit be learning how to improve their attention and concentration during study. By training themselves to concentrate better, they get better results from study without necessarily increasing their study time.

To see if you could benefit from the sections on Improving Concentration, answer the following checklist about your concentration patterns.

"HE MAY HAVE A PH.D. IN ELEMENTARY PARTICLE PHYSICS, BUT HE'S HAVING AN AWFUL LOT OF TROUBLE WITH THE APPLICATION FORM."

| Yes | No | |
|---|---|---|
| ❑ | ❑ | 1. I have the attention span of a flea. (Sorry about that! Please feel free to answer "No" even if you do wish you could concentrate better.) |
| ❑ | ❑ | 2. Daydreaming during study is a problem for me. |
| ❑ | ❑ | 3. I frequently read a page or two before realizing that although my eyes were moving across the lines, my mind was somewhere else. |
| ❑ | ❑ | 4. During study I frequently find myself thinking about personal worries. |
| ❑ | ❑ | 5. I have trouble concentrating on my studies for more than about 15 minutes at a time. |
| ❑ | ❑ | 6. My concentration span is pretty good but I'm always interested in learning ways to improve it. |
| ❑ | ❑ | 7. I am an adult student returning to school. |

If you answered "No" to each of these items, please go to **12** .

If you answered "Yes" to one or more of the items, please go to **9** .

**9**

## Improving Concentration

If you answered "Yes" to some of the above items, or are an adult student returning to school, this is the right place for you. Most students can polish their concentration abilities, and adults returning to school mention concentration difficulties as a common problem.

Some of the strategies discussed earlier in this chapter on increasing motivation and interest will also help your concentration. If you successfully develop more motivation for study and interest in your subjects, you will find that you have an easier time concentrating. Besides developing more motivation and interest, you can also do a number of things to help improve your concentration. Some strategies which have worked for many students like yourself are presented overleaf.

**Strategy 1: Minimizing External Distractions**
Remember back in Chapter 1 when we talked about choosing a quiet place for study free of interruptions or distractions? Not only is this the first step in developing an effective study routine, it is also the first step in helping improve concentration.

The physical environment you choose for study can help or hinder your concentration abilities. If your study area has poor lighting, is noisy, or is too hot or cold, your ability to concentrate will suffer. Try to choose a study place which will minimize external distractions. It's probably not a good idea to face a window during study. It may not be a good idea to study in the common study area of a library (especially if you are distracted every time someone walks by).

In some cases, it may just not be possible to find the ideal place to study. Do the best you can under these circumstances by trying to ignore sounds and sights which are distracting. Refuse to look up or give the distractions your attention. With practice, you'll find that you become more able to tune out unavoidable distractions.

**Strategy 2: Look After Your Body First**
The old maxim "A healthy body, a healthy mind" certainly applies to peak concentration. Taking good care of your body is the essential foundation for ensuring top mental performance. Enough sleep, proper nutrition, and adequate physical exercise are all essential requirements for good mental concentration. Exercise can be an especially good concentration builder. As suggested before, a short study break for some exercise can help you relax and clear your mind of tensions.

**Strategy 3: Controlling Intruding Thoughts**
Learning to control and reduce thoughts which intrude on your concentration can also be a powerful strategy for increasing concentration. It's natural for our minds to wander. Thoughts come and go like drifting clouds. When we stop and attend to every random thought, concentration suffers.

On first inspection, you might think the spontaneously occurring thoughts which interfere with concentration are beyond your control. Studies have shown, however, that we can learn to eliminate and control these intruding thoughts. One procedure which has proven especially effective is "Thought Stopping."

In "Thought Stopping," whenever you notice yourself paying attention to an intruding thought, you simply visualize the mental image of a STOP sign and say the word "STOP" subvocally to yourself. (The procedure works best for some people if they actually say the word "STOP" out loud unless, of course, they are studying in a public place.)

Simple as "Thought Stopping" sounds, it really does work. **Whenever you notice an intruding thought, see the mental image of a STOP sign and say the word "STOP" to yourself. Then direct your concentration back to your studies.**

Initially, the procedure makes you more sensitive to the presence of distracting thoughts. You learn to get rid of them before they take up too much of your valuable study time. As you practise the procedure, you'll find that you have to use it less and less. You will develop increased powers of directing your concentration where you want it.

**Strategy 4: Dealing with Personal Problems**
Are personal or family problems reaching the point where they are damaging your ability to concentrate? Sometimes it can help to talk about them with someone. Chances are your school has a teacher or counsellor who could help. Don't hesitate to ask for their help.

**Strategy 5: Getting Rid of Worries**
One type of intrusive thought especially damaging to concentration is worry. During your next study session, try to notice if recurring worries are interfering with your concentration. Do you find yourself worrying about all you have to study and how little time you have? Do you worry that you'll never remember everything you should for that upcoming test? Do you spend time during study worrying about personal concerns or family problems? If so, worry may be robbing you of valuable concentration time.

Like other intrusive thoughts, worries can be minimized or eliminated by using the Thought Stopping procedure. As with other intrusive thoughts, the next time you are preoccupied by a worry during study, mentally visualize a STOP sign and say the word "STOP" to yourself. Then redirect your full attention to your work.

Another strategy is to try to get rid of your worries before you start to study. For example, many little everyday worries revolve around chores we have to do. Do you have some bills to pay, a thank you note to write, or dishes to wash? Maybe the best solution would be to make an effort to catch up on these little chores before starting to study. Then they won't be around to bug you during study.

A related way of managing worry is to use time management strategies (more on this in the next chapter). Basically, the idea is that when you recall that you have to do something, rather than worrying about it, you add the activity to a "To Do" list. Then forget about it until you have time to complete the task. Your mind is now clear to concentrate on your studies.

Research on the best ways to control worry suggests that many people find it useful to set aside a few minutes of "worry time" every day. During this time they bring all of their worries out in the open and do some "serious worrying." Many people find that this worry time helps them spend less time worrying during the rest of the day.

"I TOLD THEM THAT REFUSING TO READ DICKENS IS LIKE REFUSING TO DO ALGEBRA. NOW THEY REFUSE TO DO ALGEBRA."

If you still find yourself worrying during study, make a habit of getting up from your study desk when a worry intrudes. Go somewhere else. Spend a few minutes thinking about the worry and what you might do to solve the problem. Choose the solution that seems best and then return to your study area. The idea is to do something about your worries by seeking and acting on solutions to worrisome problems.

**Strategy 6: Respect Your Concentration Span**
Don't make the mistake of trying to study longer than your best concentration span. Do you have a good idea right now of how long you can usually concentrate before your attention wanders? If not, the next time you study, conduct your own research project to discover the length of your normal concentration span.

Note the time you start studying, then record the time when you notice your attention weakening. After doing this for several study sessions, average the time intervals to come up with the estimate of your present concentration span. (If you're a real student of human behaviour, you might also want to track how your concentration span varies related to what you're studying. The smart money predicts that your concentration span will be longer for those subjects in which you are more interested.)

If your average concentration span is less than 15 minutes, it will be especially important for you to try to lengthen your optimal span. In any case, the important thing for efficient study is that you don't try to keep working beyond your concentration span. When you've reached your concentration limit, take a short break and use it to revitalize yourself for renewed concentration.

Organizing your study time can also help. Try dividing your assignments into smaller parts, each of which can be comfortably finished within your usual ideal concentration limits. Another organizational tip for increasing concentration is to make sure that each study session contains some variety. It will be more difficult to maintain ideal concentration if you spend two hours working on the same subject than if you allocate this time to several different subjects.

**Strategy 7: Increasing Your Concentration Span**
If you can maintain good concentration for 40 to 50 minutes at a stretch, you really don't have a problem. If your usual concentration span is lower than 30 minutes, you could probably benefit

by increasing it. Fortunately, you can train yourself to increase your concentration span.

The strategy for increasing your concentration span is very straightforward. Start by only working as long as your average good concentration span, then gradually work on increasing it. When you've reached your span, take a short break, then come back for more study. The next time you sit down to study, plan to increase your concentration span by a few minutes. Work this longer time, then take your short study break. After a week or so of gradually increasing your periods of concentration, sitting down and concentrating for longer times will come quite naturally.

**Strategy 8: Use Active Learning to Increase Concentration**
Actively vary your study strategies to help refocus your concentration. When you notice your concentration weakening, maybe it would help to stop reading at that point and refocus your attention on trying to summarize or review what you have read so far. Another strategy of active involvement is to always have a pen or pencil in your hand and use it to underline, highlight important points, or to make notes. Or, if you find your attention flagging after reading for ten or fifteen minutes, you might pause for a few minutes and look over the headings and illustrations in the rest of the chapter you are reading. Ask yourself some questions about what you are likely to learn in the rest of the chapter, then resume reading to find the answers.

The common element behind each of these suggestions is that anything you do during study which makes you more actively involved in the learning process is also likely to help you focus your concentration on learning. Can you think of anything else you could be doing during study to make you more actively involved?

**Strategy 9: Maintain Balance in Your Life**
For those students who have families or are working in addition to taking courses, maintaining balance in your life will probably take care of itself. But if you are a full time student, remember that there is such a thing as too much of a good thing. Don't spend all of your free time studying. Make sure that your life contains activities which offer a contrast to studying. If your life is varied, you'll be more able to concentrate effectively when you do study.

☞ go to **11**

## 10

You're here because you just finished reading about ways to make your studies more interesting. Frankly, just reading about these strategies won't do much good. It's time to translate some of these tips into action!

You can review the ideas presented in section **7**, if necessary. Then decide which strategies appeal most to you and which ones might be most helpful. Use the following space to record ways you will be working to become more interested in coursework and studying.

**Strategies I will try:**

1.______________________________________________
________________________________________________
________________________________________________
________________________________________________

2.______________________________________________
________________________________________________
________________________________________________
________________________________________________

3.______________________________________________
________________________________________________
________________________________________________
________________________________________________

**Examples of how I will apply these strategies, to what courses, etc.:**

________________________________________________
________________________________________________
________________________________________________
________________________________________________
________________________________________________
________________________________________________
________________________________________________
________________________________________________
________________________________________________
________________________________________________
________________________________________________
________________________________________________
________________________________________________
________________________________________________
________________________________________________
________________________________________________
________________________________________________

Use an extra sheet of paper if you need more room. The important thing is to work out a game plan. It should spell out in detail what you are going to try, and how you will do it. Writing out your plans makes it much more likely that you will follow through with them. After several weeks, it may be a good idea to return to this page to remind yourself of your goals and to rekindle your efforts at becoming more interested in your coursework.

When you've finished, please go to **8**.

**11**

Section **9** had a number of tips for helping improve and lengthen your concentration span. If necessary, go back there and review the tips for improving your concentration during study. What strategies would seem most helpful to you? How could you best apply these strategies to your own study patterns? After you've had a chance to think about these questions, develop your own personal plan to improve your concentration. Use the space below to outline your plan.

**I plan to increase my ability to concentrate by:**

-----------------------------------------------

-----------------------------------------------

-----------------------------------------------

-----------------------------------------------

-----------------------------------------------

-----------------------------------------------

-----------------------------------------------

-----------------------------------------------

-----------------------------------------------

-----------------------------------------------

-----------------------------------------------

-----------------------------------------------

-----------------------------------------------

Please go back and fill out your "concentration plan" if you skipped it. The little bit of extra thought and effort required to do so will dramatically increase the likelihood that you will later be motivated to apply these strategies to your studies.

If you've completed your "concentration plan" go to **12** .

**12**

Chapter 2 examined various strategies which have been successfully used by other students to become more motivated and interested in their studies and to increase study efficiency by improving concentration abilities.

Studies have shown that very good students naturally use many of these techniques to get the most out of their study time. Other students can also learn to apply these strategies to "study smarter without studying harder."

That's all for Chapter 2. Come back and visit us occasionally. Sections **4** , **10** and **11** would especially appreciate a return visit whenever you would like to remind yourself of your plans for becoming more motivated, interested, and attentive to your studies. Thanks for the visit.

Time now for a goofing-off break. When you're ready to come back, either continue to Chapter 3 or go to another chapter that looks interesting.

# CHAPTER 3
# Making the Most of Your Time

**In this chapter you can learn**

- *how to find time for study*
- *how to make the best use of your study time*
- *how to avoid putting things off*

"What, of all things in the world, is the longest and the shortest, the swiftest and the slowest, the most divisible and the most extended, the most neglected and the most regretted, without which nothing can be done, which devours all that is little, and enlivens all that is great?"

*Voltaire*

You've probably guessed that the answer is "Time." Using your time effectively is an important student survival strategy. Students who do well in school find time for necessary study and they use that time efficiently. How do you stack up? Do you have problems finding enough time for study? Could you make wiser use of your time? Answer this checklist to see if you could benefit from the survival strategies of Chapter 3.

| Yes | No | |
|---|---|---|
| ❑ | ❑ | 1. I often have difficulty finding enough time for study. |
| ❑ | ❑ | 2. Family responsibilities leave little extra time for study. |
| ❑ | ❑ | 3. I work part-time or full-time in addition to school work. |
| ❑ | ❑ | 4. I would do better in my courses if I had more time to study. |

If you answered "Yes" to one or more of these items, go to **1**.

If you answered "No" to each of these items, you are probably already able to find sufficient time for coursework. Keep up the good work!

☞ go to **2**

**1**

## Finding Time for Study

This section will give you some ideas for finding more time for your schoolwork. (If you are an adult returning to school, the section may be especially helpful. Returning adult students report that finding enough time for study is a major problem.)

If you're serious about doing well in your courses and getting good marks, it's essential that you devote time to reaching these goals. During my years as a professor, I've spoken with many students who were trying to understand the reasons for a poor examination mark. One of my first questions is always "How long did you study for the exam?" You'd be surprised how many students report studying only a few hours for a major test. Not only had they not given themselves enough time, but they barely devoted enough time for a once-only reading of the assignments.

Making efficient use of time is an art. Few of us come by it naturally. Unless you are careful, your daily schedule can be filled with low priority activities. When this happens, not enough time is left for higher priority activities like studying.

Finding enough time for study can be even more difficult when you cope with trying to lead a well balanced life. A balanced life should include enough time for sleep, family and social activities, relaxation, and exercise still leaving enough time for coursework. If you're like most students, there never seems to be enough time for everything. What's the first step in finding more time?

**Using "T I M E" to find time**
Obviously, we can't help you create more time. What we can do is suggest that you become more aware of how you use your time. Almost always, this awareness can help you find ways to use your time more effectively. The "T I M E" survival strategy for finding more study time has four steps:

T	**Time** your activities.

I	**Inspect** how you spend your time.

M	**Monitor** your priorities.

E	**Evaluate** your plan.

**Time Your Activities**

Start by keeping a "Time Record" of how you spend each day. For each hour of the day, keep a record of how you used that time. Keep your Time Record for a full week. You'll end up knowing exactly how you spent your time.

When keeping your Time Record, it's important that you keep up your normal routine. Remember that the purpose of the Time Record is to find out how you **typically** spend your time.

As a student, your daily activities will generally fit into these categories:
1) attending class; 2) study; 3) sleeping; 4) eating; 5) travel; 6) relaxation; 7) other responsibilities (such as home, family, etc.); and 8) other work (such as a part-time or full-time job).
Use these categories to keep your Time Record.

Use the chart in Box 3 to record your Time Record for one week.

Box 3

**Time Record**

| Hour | Monday | Tuesday | Wednesday | Thursday | Friday | Saturday | Sunday |
|---|---|---|---|---|---|---|---|
| 7:00-8:00 | | | | | | | |
| 8:00-9:00 | | | | | | | |
| 9:00-10:00 | | | | | | | |
| 10:00-11:00 | | | | | | | |
| 11:00-12:00 | | | | | | | |
| 12:00-1:00 | | | | | | | |
| 1:00-2:00 | | | | | | | |
| 2:00-3:00 | | | | | | | |
| 3:00-4:00 | | | | | | | |
| 4:00-5:00 | | | | | | | |
| 5:00-6:00 | | | | | | | |
| 6:00-7:00 | | | | | | | |
| 7:00-8:00 | | | | | | | |
| 8:00-9:00 | | | | | | | |
| 9:00-10:00 | | | | | | | |
| 10:00-11:00 | | | | | | | |
| 11:00-12:00 | | | | | | | |
| 12:00-7:00 | | | | | | | |

**Inspect How You Spend Your Time**

The second step in finding more study time is to inspect your Time Record. Try to get an overall view of how your spend your time. When you have a Time Record for one week, use Box 4 to find out how much time you are spending on each activity.

When you have completed the time summaries in Box 4, take a look at your time patterns. There are a number of ways to look for patterns. For example, you might take each day and assign the activities a rank based on how much time was spent on it. Sleep will probably have the largest times, so it would be assigned a rank of "1." The activity taking the next largest block of time would be assigned a rank of "2" and so on till you reach the activity ranked as "8." Try this ranking for each day, and also for the weekly totals.

Look for other patterns. It's likely, for example, that more time will be spent on relaxation during the weekend than during the week. How do the times you spend on study and relaxation during the week compare with each other? Are your study times fairly constant on each day or do they vary? Does study tend to occur during the same times on each day? Do you see any blocks of time which could be used for other activities?

Looking at your Time Record summary with these questions in mind will help set the stage for you to better match your time to your priorities.

**Monitor Your Priorities**

At this point in your T I M E plan, you know how you spend a typical week. In order to find more time for your schoolwork, you will have to spend less time on other activities. This "found" time can then be applied to your studies. One way to "find" this time is to monitor your priorities.

Your priorities should be arranged before you settle on how you will manage your time more effectively. To use your time to your best advantage, it is important that you give time to activities so that the time spent matches the priority of that activity. In other words, how much time you spend on an activity should reflect how much you value that activity.

Because you are a student, your studies probably have a reasonably high priority in your life. If you need more study time or if your total study time does not reflect your priorities for doing well in your courses, you'll have to find more time for study. This time will come from other lower priority activities.

Box 4

**Time Record Summary**

Go back to your Time Record and add up the total times you spent on each activity for the entire week. Don't worry about exact minutes, just round to the nearest half hour.

| Activity | Monday Hours | Tuesday Hours | Wednesday Hours | Thursday Hours | Friday Hours | Saturday Hours | Sunday Hours | Total Hours |
|---|---|---|---|---|---|---|---|---|
| 1. Class | | | | | | | | |
| 2. Study | | | | | | | | |
| 3. Sleep | | | | | | | | |
| 4. Eat | | | | | | | | |
| 5. Travel | | | | | | | | |
| 6. Relax | | | | | | | | |
| 7. Other | | | | | | | | |
| 8. Work | | | | | | | | |

If you are like the majority of full-time students, your Time Record may suggest that more study time can be found by making modest reductions in relaxation time. Although you probably find relaxation more fun than studying, relaxation should have a lower priority. We all need a certain amount of relaxation, but not at the expense of higher priority activities.

Taking time from one activity and giving it to another can be a difficult choice. If you are an adult student, for example, your family responsibilities have a high priority. Taking time from these family duties may not be practical or desirable. Yet, some hard decisions will have to be made if you are to find the study time necessary to succeed in your role as a student.

When you are trying to find time for study and managing your time to match your priorities, keep these suggestions in mind:

• When you need more time for a high priority activity, always try to "find" the time by reducing time spent on lower priority activities.

• Experiment with ways to reduce the time spent on low priority, routine activities. For example, if you usually take an hour or more"to get going" in the morning, try to cut this time in half by skipping that second cup of coffee, spending less time in the bathroom, picking out your clothes the night before, etc.

• Get all the sleep you need to function at your best but don't spend more time sleeping than you need. People generally require from 6 to 8 hours of sleep although some can get by on less.

Do you know how much sleep you need to function at your best? If you're sleeping 8 or more hours a day and are pressed for more time to get things done, try a little experiment. Reduce your daily sleeping time by a half hour and see what happens. If you don't notice any difference, chances are you didn't need this extra half hour of sleep. You've "found" an extra half hour! If, however, you notice that you are tired and not at your best after a few days of reduced sleep, go back to your longer sleeping times.

• Be ruthless in spotting wasted time! Do you use that break between classes for study or do you use it to join your friends at Seven-Eleven? Do you find yourself relaxing before you study rather than after? Do you spend too much time reading the daily newspaper? Try and develop the habit of spotting wasted time and keeping it to a low level.

• Find times when you could be doing two things at once. (Don't try it while you're driving or attending class!) There may be other times, however, when you could be getting more out of your time. If you take the bus to school, for example, why not try and use some of this travel time for study, review, or planning? Could you be reading a textbook during lunch?

• Use odd times for study. When you're waiting to see the dentist or waiting for class to start, use those few extra minutes for study. Even if you don't have your book with you you could use the time to think about what you have been learning. Better yet, have your book and notes with you and use these short blocks of "extra" time for review. It's not hard to find at least 10 to 15 minutes of this extra time every day. If you do, it can add up to an extra hour and fifteen minutes of study time by the time the weekend rolls around.

• Be willing to reorganize your priorities in a crunch. When you need that extra study time, routine cleaning may seem far less important than usual. The pressures of an upcoming exam may decrease your enjoyment of a "regular" TV show. Social interactions may have to take a temporary back seat to study.

• In spite of it all, try for balance in how you spend your time. Rest and relaxation are important. Try for one day during the weekend when (except for emergencies) you do not study. The break will do you good. Do, however, monitor your relaxation time. Don't let it get out of hand at the expense of your studies.

• Use all of these tips and any others you can think of if you also work at another job besides being a student. Working either part-time or full-time while you are also taking courses can test your powers of time management. It will be especially important for you to find extra time for study. With so little free time, you will have to pay special effort to not wasting any potential study time. Develop your own individual plan by using the strategies in this chapter that seem most appropriate to you.

**Evaluate Your Efforts**

Old habits often die hard. Many students find that after they conduct their Time Record and find extra time for study, they gradually fall back into their old habits. The only surefire way to prevent this is to periodically evaluate your efforts. If you sense that you are reverting back to former inefficient uses of time, it would be a good idea to go through the T I M E plan again. Do your Time Record again, check the results, and make necessary changes or improvements in how you are using your time.

When evaluating your time management efforts, don't forget to recognize your achievements. Feel good about managing time more efficiently. Give yourself a pat on the back for spotting time wasters and using time more productively.

Don't lose track of the fact that time management should be fun. Time management will help you get your school work under control. When you're in control, an activity is more enjoyable. Time management can also help make leisure time more enjoyable. Having your studies completed, you can relax and have fun without worrying about coursework.

☞ go to **2**

**2**

Time for another check-up. Please think about your own study patterns and answer the checklist items as they apply to you.

| Yes | No | |
|---|---|---|
| ☐ | ☐ | 1. I sometimes forget about course assignments. |
| ☐ | ☐ | 2. I have a weekly study plan which schedules my study time. |
| ☐ | ☐ | 3. I spend a few minutes every day planning the day's study schedule. |
| ☐ | ☐ | 4. I have regular times during the day which are reserved for study. |
| ☐ | ☐ | 5. I organize my study sessions to best cope with course demands and my concentration span. |
| ☐ | ☐ | 6. I plan for "emergency" study time I might need. |
| ☐ | ☐ | 7. I schedule some time during every study session for review. |

If you answered "Yes" to each of these items, consider becoming a time-management expert!

Engaging in all of the checklist activities means you are probably highly efficient in scheduling adequate study time. (This assumes, of course, that you actually follow your schedule!) Unless you are interested in seeing possible ways you might improve your present time management scheduling, you can skip section **3** .

☞ go to **4**

If you answered "No" to some of the checklist items, the chances are good that the following section will give you some useful survival tips.

☞ go to **3**

**3**

## Making the Best Use of Your Time

This section will give you some ideas for making better use of your study time. Most students find that planning and scheduling study times is very helpful. Study skills specialists agree. A little thought to planning and individualizing your study schedule can pay big dividends.

The "P L A N" Survival Strategy can let you develop the time management skills which will help you get more out of your studies.

"P L A N" looks like this:

**P** **Put** assignments in your date diary

**L** **Lay** out a study schedule

**A** **Analyse** your schedule

**N** **Navigate** to success

## Put Assignments in Your Date Diary

The first step in organizing your study schedule is to make sure you have an assignment date diary. Unless you are lucky enough to have a photographic memory, you're going to have to write your assignments down to remember them.

Student assignment diaries are available in office supply stores, bookstores, and the stationery sections of department stores. They are generally small enough so that you can carry them with you (a good idea), and have enough space for each day of the school year to record assignment due dates and exams.

If you don't have an assignment diary, get one. It's a super way to begin planning your school year. Once you've entered all assignment and test dates, you'll be able to see at a glance all of your important deadlines.

Once you have your diary, use it. Some instructors give a course outline at the beginning of classes. These outlines usually specify all assignments and tests for the course. Transfer this information from the outline to your assignment diary. (Save the outline with your course notes.)

Other instructors may not give an outline, but they will announce in advance when assignments are due and test dates. Copy this information down in your course notes and also be sure to enter it into your assignment diary.

If your assignment diary has enough room, also enter important details of each assignment or test. (If you don't have room in your diary for this, be sure you get this information written down in your class notes.) Include page numbers for reading assignments, titles and page numbers for extra readings, problems or exercises to be completed for labs, material to be covered on tests, essay topics and due dates, and any special instructions or tips from your teacher.

The important thing is to get these things written down. It will help you complete your course work with less difficulty. Try to make sure that your assignment diary is always complete and up-to-date. Get into the habit of looking at it every day. Look ahead to see what's coming up. Then an assignment or test date will never catch you by surprise.

## Lay Out a Study Schedule

The second step of P L A N is to lay out a study schedule. Some tips which can help you plan a weekly study schedule include:

- Start by looking ahead in your assignment diary. Notice any important assignments or tests which are approaching. Use this information to help you plan the week's study priorities.
- Spend a little time organizing and planning your week before making your study schedule. Try to work in study time for each of your courses. Look for extra time to give to special assignments or upcoming examinations.
- Try to block out regular times every day which are reserved for study.
- Reserve blocks of time as "extra study." Use this time if you have to, otherwise do something else. This scheduling trick gives you extra study time which can be used for emergencies (if you need more study for an upcoming test, if you've missed an earlier study time, if you're falling behind in a course, etc.)
- If a test is approaching, allow yourself extra time for "cramming."
- Reserve a small block of time every day to spend reviewing previous learning. This will end up producing some of your most valuable study time!
- Don't forget to schedule short breaks into your study schedule.
- Specify on your weekly study schedule how you will spend each block of study time. For example, don't just write down "study" in the 7:00 to 9:00 Monday evening times. Be specific. If you're going to divide the time between math and history, put it on your schedule that way.

In addition to their weekly study schedule, some students make an additional daily schedule. Their weekly schedule gives the "big picture" of how they will spend their study time for the week. The daily schedule is used to set the immediate goals for each study session. In some ways, their daily study schedule is like a "To Do" list. It may contain items like "Study chemistry for 45 minutes. (Spend 10 minutes reviewing class notes. Spend 35 minutes studying Chapter 5)." and so on for each activity during the study session.

Students who use both the weekly schedule and the daily schedule tend to be the best organized. Their weekly schedule helps keep things in perspective and the daily To Do schedule breaks their work into small workable tasks.

When finished with one of these tasks, these students strike it off their list. At the end of the study session, they have a clear picture of what was accomplished.

One last (but important) word about the value of study schedules. They **will** help you become a better and more efficient learner! Study schedules represent your learning goals. As such, they help motivate you, help target and focus your concentration, and keep your efforts on track. In a way, your study schedule becomes a "contract" with yourself. Honoring this contract will help you become a more efficient student.

**Analyse Your Schedule**
The third step of P L A N involves analysing your study schedules. The purpose of this analysis is to see if your personal study schedule gives you the best chance of "studying smarter, not harder."

After several weeks of study scheduling, pull out your old schedules and have a look at them. Keep the following tips in mind when you are fine-tuning your study schedule.

- Have I given myself enough study time to reach my own learning goals and the course requirements?
- Have I planned work early enough to comfortably meet deadlines?
- Have I included review periods in my schedule?
- Have I included breaks in my schedule?
- Have I used blocks of study time which do not exceed my best concentration span?
- Have I reserved some time for extra study if needed?
- Have I scheduled regular time blocks for study?
- Have I set realistic study goals for each study session?
- Do I reward myself for meeting my study goals?
- Is my schedule flexible? If I miss a necessary study time, is there room in my schedule to fit it in somewhere else?
- Do I use my "peak times" to study difficult or non-preferred courses?
- Do I vary subjects within each study session?
- Do I stop working when my concentration reaches the point of "diminishing returns"?
- After studying a subject, do I work next on a subject which is quite different from the first one? (Doing this introduces variety, which can help with concentration.)
- Do I review material shortly before going to sleep? (Studies show this helps memory.)
- Have I done a reasonably good job in following my study schedule?

Each of these features has been shown to improve study efficiency. Analyse your own study schedules and see how you compare. If you notice room for improvements, make them!

**Navigate to Success**
The final step of P L A N is to use your schedule to help navigate to success. It's been said that if you don't know where you're going, you'll never get there. A carefully designed study schedule can be a powerful "navigational" aid. It reflects your goals and priorities. It spells out what you will do to reach your objectives. It also breaks your journey into easily reached sub-destinations.

Remember, once you develop the habit of following your study schedule, you'll have an automatic edge on all the students who fail to use this powerful organizational strategy!

☞ go to **4**

**4**

In the final section of this chapter we're going to examine a topic near and dear to the hearts of most students—procrastination. It's been called "the student's disease" and teachers think of it as an epidemic! (In case you don't recognize the word, "procrastination" refers to the tendency to habitually put off doing things until the last possible moment.)

Although most students show some procrastination, it can cause problems if it becomes a habit. To see if you could benefit by learning new ways to reduce procrastination, answer the following checklist.

| Yes | No | |
|---|---|---|
| ❑ | ❑ | 1. I cram for exams. |
| ❑ | ❑ | 2. Rather than starting study or an assignment now, I often find myself saying, "I'll do it tomorrow." |
| ❑ | ❑ | 3. I often find myself putting off doing coursework or study until the last possible moment. |

☐ ☐ 4. I sometime have trouble getting started on a "big project."

☐ ☐ 5. My schoolwork tends to pile up on me.

☐ ☐ 6. I am taking a correspondence course(s).

☐ ☐ 7. I set very high standards for my own work.

If you answered "No" to each of these items, procrastination is probably not causing you any difficulties.

☞ go to 6

If you answered "Yes" to one or more of these items, procrastination may be robbing you of the chance to be a higher achieving student. You can probably benefit from the tips and strategies of section 5.

☞ go to 5

**5**

## Conquering Procrastination

If you're like most students, there are probably times when you put off your study or assignments until the last possible moment. (Procrastination is especially common among correspondence students. Putting coursework off can become a bad habit when you don't have the pressure of regular classes or the teacher reminding your of assignments every day.) All of the time management strategies of this chapter can help you reduce procrastination (if you use them). In addition, you may find the "N O W" anti-procrastination plan helpful.

"N O W" looks like this:

N **Narrow** the task

O **Organize** yourself

W **Wonder** why you ever procrastinated.

**Narrow the Task**

One of the major causes of procrastination among students is the feeling that an assignment or goal is just too big. When you have a complex and difficult job ahead of you, it's only natural that you'll tend to put it off. It's much easier to find anything else to do rather than dig into what you feel will be a big job. Narrowing your coursework and study into smaller tasks can reduce the temptation to procrastinate.

When you are doing your weekly study schedule, always try to set reasonable goals. Don't block out three hours of study if you know that you can never stand more than two hours. Set a study goal which you can reasonably expect to attain without it being unpleasant.

When blocking out your study schedule, try to break every reading or work assignment into small manageable tasks. As an example, let's suppose you have been putting off starting work on an essay. You may not like to write and you see the essay as a "big" project. Try thinking about it as several smaller projects, rather than as one large assignment.

Block out some time to just look over your notes on what is expected for the essay. Then spend a little time thinking about a possible topic that would be most interesting to you. Once you've selected a topic you're rolling! You've taken that first step. When you have a topic in mind your efforts will be more directed and purposeful (and easier). Proceed to another small step when you have time. Maybe the next step would involve going to the library to check out a few references on your essay topic. You don't have to read the references now, just check them out and bring them to your study area so they are ready for you. You get the idea. By breaking the assignment into smaller chunks, they become more manageable and get you started.

Get into the habit of using the "Divide and Conquer" strategy to set "easy" goals for yourself. Each sub task then becomes simpler and quicker. When you have an easy task facing you, getting at it right "N O W" becomes more attractive.

**Organize Yourself**

All of the time management strategies discussed earlier in this chapter can help you overcome procrastination. Getting organized plays a big part. By setting small, manageable goals, you organize yourself for action. Many students have also found the following tips helpful:

- Make a study schedule. Use this organizational and planning aid to help focus your efforts and get you started.
- Schedule **regular** study time. Get into the habit of using these regular times for "high quality" work.
- Don't let your work pile up. Too much goofing off and the work builds to the point where you dread starting. Keep up with your coursework by doing a little every day.
- Start your study session by working on your least preferred or most difficult subject. Get it out of the way while you're fresh. This will help you develop the habit of not procrastinating.
- When you find yourself procrastinating, treat yourself to a motivational "pep" talk.
- Plan ahead. Give yourself plenty of time to complete work assignments.
- Plan a reasonable study schedule every day and try to stick to it.
- Do a "Balance Sheet" analysis of a task you have been delaying. Write down all the benefits of delaying and all the benefits of getting the task done. The benefits of completing the task will usually far outweigh the excuses for delaying.
- Assign priorities to everything on your daily "To Do" list. Low priority tasks can slide from one day to the next. However, try to develop the habit of always completing the high priority items today.

**Wonder Why You Ever Procrastinated**

The time management strategies presented in this chapter can help you develop the powerful habit of doing your school work "N O W." Once you develop this habit, you'll wonder how you ever tolerated procrastination.

As you gradually get into the habit of avoiding procrastination, don't forget to take stock of your accomplishments. Feel good about getting an assignment done as you planned! Doesn't it beat worrying about something that is hanging over your head? Use the self-motivation strategies discussed earlier and the tips from this chapter to help get yourself moving. You'll be a more efficient student because of your efforts!

## 6

Those of you who have worked through sections of this chapter have learned strategies which can help you make more efficient use of time and become a more efficient student. Please don't just read about these strategies. Pick those which seem most appropriate to your own needs and start applying them to your own life. Develop your own personal "game plan" and use your plan to help you study smarter, not harder.

If you've skipped all of this chapter, it should be because you already are highly organized, have enough time for study, make the most efficient use of your time, and don't procrastinate. Are you sure? It almost sounds too good to be true. Feel free to go back and look at parts of this chapter just to make sure you haven't missed something which could help you study smarter, not harder.

It's probably time for a break now. Come back later and look at another chapter which looks interesting.

COLLEGE
OF
ARTS & SCIENCES
(AND A FEW THINGS
TO FALL BACK ON)
S. Harris

# CHAPTER 4
# Reading and Remembering

**In this chapter you can learn**

- *how to get more out of your reading*
- *how to improve your memory*

"I took a speed reading course, learning to read straight down the middle of the page and I was able to go through War and Peace in twenty minutes. It's about Russia."

*Woody Allen*

This chapter won't teach you how to read as fast as Woody Allen, but it will share powerful learning strategies which can help make you a more efficient reader. Your ability to read and remember makes a major contribution to your success as a student and lifelong learner. To see if you could benefit from the strategies presented in this chapter, answer the following checklist.

| Yes | No | |
|---|---|---|
| ❑ | ❑ | 1. I often read a textbook in much the same way that I read a novel or newspaper. |
| ❑ | ❑ | 2. I often have difficulty picking out the main ideas in a textbook. |
| ❑ | ❑ | 3. I usually read an assigned chapter straight through from the first to the last page. |
| ❑ | ❑ | 4. I seldom stop to reread a part I didn't understand. (Mark "Yes" if this applies to you. Mark "No" if you stop to reread difficult passages.) |
| ❑ | ❑ | 5. I seldom try to see how a reading assignment is personally relevant to me. (Mark "Yes" if this applies to you. Mark "No" if you try to make assignments personally relevant.) |
| ❑ | ❑ | 6. My coursework would probably benefit if I read more effectively. |
| ❑ | ❑ | 7. I wish I could remember more of what I've read. |

If you answered "No" to each of these items, you've probably already developed an adequate reading approach for effective study. If you're interested in further improvements in your reading efficiency, have a look at section **1**. Otherwise, go to **2**.

If you answered "Yes" to one or more of the items, you can benefit by learning (and using) the reading strategies presented in this chapter.

☞ go to **1**

**1**

## Reading for Active Learning

Your success as a student depends heavily on reading proficiency. The study strategies presented here are designed to help you read for understanding and memory. They assume that you already have "average" reading skills. The tips in this chapter will help you use your present reading skills and apply them so you can study smarter.

If your present reading skills are weak, or if you are learning English as a second language, you'll need more help than this chapter can provide. Reading courses are available in many parts of the province. A local high school should be able to give you information on courses in your area. If you are a college student, see a college counsellor or learning skills specialist to find out what programs are available for improving reading skills.

Earlier we suggested that learning is best when you are an active learner. This section will show you how to apply the principle of Active Learning to reading and study.

### Reading for Different Purposes

The purpose for reading should influence how you read. Good students read a textbook very differently than they read an entertaining Stephen King novel. Recreational reading is usually faster. You are not as concerned with remembering or understanding. In recreational reading, you usually start at the beginning and read straight through to the end. When reading a novel for enjoyment, you seldom return and reread a previous passage.

Unfortunately, many students apply this reading style to their coursework. As if they were reading a novel, they read from beginning to end without trying to become actively involved in increasing their understanding and memory for what they have just read.

Have you ever noticed how much you remember about an entertaining novel a month later? If you're like most readers, you'll be doing well to even remember the plot. Reading a textbook like you read a novel will give the same results. Nearly everything you've read in a text will be rapidly forgotten unless you learn to read for understanding and memory. Fortunately, help is in sight. Read on.

**"Power Study" with SQ3R**

Hundreds of studies of the most effective way to learn and remember point to a similar finding. We learn best when we are actively involved. One of the most powerful strategies for increasing active learning is the "SQ3R" method. (SQ3R is a shorthand way of remembering the five steps.) The steps of SQ3R are:

| | |
|---|---|
| **S** | **Survey** |
| **Q** | **Question** |
| **R** | **Read** |
| **R** | **Recite** |
| **R** | **Review** |

As you can see, reading is only one of the five SQ3R steps for effective study. Let's look at each part of the SQ3R study method and see how you can apply it to your own learning.

**Survey**

So, what's the first thing you do when faced with a reading assignment? Read? Wrong! You'll give yourself a powerful edge by first making a Survey of what you will read.

The idea behind making a survey is to see what the forest looks like before you march into the trees. See the big picture before digging into details. Making an initial survey is an easy habit to develop because we already naturally survey most of our recreational reading. When reading a newspaper, for example, most of us will first survey the headline. We use this survey to decide if we will read all, part, or none of the story.

Your study should also begin with a survey. What should you be looking for? Start by making a short survey of the entire textbook. This doesn't have to be a time consuming task. Spend a few minutes seeing how the book is organized. Discover the major topics covered in the book. See how material is presented within each chapter.

In making an initial survey of a textbook, here are some things you might look for:

*Making a Survey of a Textbook*

- Look at the title page. What is the title of the book? What are the names of the authors? When was the book published? What is the general subject area?
- Look at the Preface. Some authors may call it the Introduction or the Foreword. Scan this section. See if the author tells you why the book was written and for whom.
- Scan the Contents page. This page will tell you what the book deals with. It will give you an idea of how the book is organized.
- Quickly leaf through the book. Read the chapter headings and note any subheadings.
- If the book has summaries at the end of the chapters, read them.
- Look at any illustrations, graphs, or pictures.
- Notice if the book has a glossary of terms at the end.

Your textbook survey will pay dividends later on. After a few minutes surveying a text, you'll have a general impression of the contents and will be better prepared for later learning.

Before you start studying a text chapter, you should also survey the chapter. Your chapter survey will be more detailed than the survey of the entire book. Some of the things to look for when making a chapter survey include:

*Making a Chapter Survey*

- Notice the chapter title.
- Some textbooks present a summary outline of the chapter contents at the beginning of each chapter (or learning objectives). If present, read this information.
- Read the first and last paragraphs of each chapter if the author uses them to overview what is to come or to summarize the chapter.
- Read anything labelled as a summary.
- Read the headings and subheadings. Authors use them to organize major ideas. Headings and subheadings tell you what topics will be dealt with in each section of the chapter.
- Notice the relative sizes of various headings and subheadings. More important topics usually have larger headings.
- Notice any words appearing in bold print. Authors frequently indicate important concepts or definitions by using bold type.
- Look at any figures, illustrations, graphs, or photographs. Read the captions.

How long should you spend doing a survey of a textbook chapter? There are no fixed rules. Most students find that 10 minutes or so is enough to do a reasonably good survey of the average chapter. At the end of your chapter survey you'll have a pretty good idea of what you'll be learning from the chapter. At this point you've taken the first step toward becoming a more active learner.

**Question**

The second step of the SQ3R plan is to ask yourself questions about what you are going to read. Your survey has already given you a general impression of what the chapter is about. Use this impression to ask yourself some questions.

The intent is to become more actively involved during reading. When you ask questions beforehand, your reading has a purpose. You are now reading to find the answers to your own questions. Active reading generates more interest and focuses your attention. It also increases the chances that you will remember what you have read. Text material which answers your questions will stick in your memory.

It's a good idea to never begin a detailed reading of a text without first formulating a set of questions. Use what you have learned from your survey to pose your questions. Some students find it helpful to actually combine the survey and question steps. They write down questions at the same time or shortly after the survey.

Keep these "question words" in mind as you pose questions: Who, What, Where, When, Why, and How. See Box 5 on this page for examples of the types of questions which might be suggested by a chapter survey.

Box 5

**Using Your Chapter Survey to Generate Questions**

Here are some examples of how you might use your survey of a text chapter to ask questions about what you are about to read.

- **Use the chapter title to ask questions** Your questions might look like this: "What is the main topic of this chapter?" "Why is the material in this chapter important?" "How does the material in this chapter relate to what I already know?"

- **Use section headings and subheadings to suggest questions** For example, when you saw the heading "Power Study with SQ3R," you might have asked questions like: "What is Power Study?" "What is SQ3R?" "How can SQ3R lead to power study?" or "What can Power Study do for me?" With a little practice, headings will automatically suggest questions. If all else fails, ask yourself "What does this heading mean?"

- **Ask questions about figures, graphs, and photographs** When you see these illustrations, ask yourself questions like: "What variables are shown in this graph?" "How are the variables in the graph related to each other?" "What does the graph mean?" "What does this photograph illustrate?" "How is this photograph related to the concepts discussed in the text?" or "What main idea is illustrated in this diagram?"

- **Use summaries to ask questions about main ideas** Use summaries or learning objectives (if present) to ask questions about the main ideas. Focus your questions on how the main ideas are most relevant to you. For example, the two learning objectives at the beginning of this chapter might lead to questions such as: "How can I learn to get more out of my reading?" "What will I have to do?" "Is there anything about my current reading habits which could be improved?" "How can I study for better understanding and memory?" "What's wrong with what I'm doing now?" You get the idea. If your questions are related to how the material might be of most use to you, your motivation, interest, and study efficiency will improve.

- **Notice definitions and ask yourself questions about them** An important part of most courses involves learning the meaning of special concepts and terms. Every time you see such a definition ask yourself a question about it. These questions can be as basic as "What is an atom?" or "How would I define climate?"

You might consider several methods of asking questions and decide upon the one that seems best for you. Some students find that writing out their questions works best. These written questions become part of their class notes and on occasion they are reviewed. Other students like to ask questions as they read. When they come to a section heading or subheading, they pause for a few seconds and ask themselves questions about the upcoming section. The questioning session is then repeated for every new section. Experiment with both methods and see which one works best for you.

Don't overlook questions which may by included in your textbook. Some authors include these to help your study. You should pay special attention to them because they highlight important parts of the chapter.

Some students who write out their questions use an additional strategy to make their questions more useful. After they have read the chapter, they return to their question sheet. Looking over their questions, they decide which ones are most important and mark these with an asterisk. This little strategy helps them concentrate on more important information.

Besides giving a purpose to your reading, asking questions helps you actively process the information you read. The mental processing that occurs when you decide if material answers a question increases your engagement in learning. The net result of the whole effort is that you end up with improved understanding and memory.

Once you've asked yourself questions about what you will read, you are now ready to begin a careful reading of the material.

**Read**

The third step of the SQ3R method involves a careful reading of the material. Unlike most of your casual reading, you will now be reading for a purpose. You already have a general idea of what you will be reading. You have asked yourself questions. This preparation will set the stage for "Power Reading."

Power reading is like a treasure hunt in which you search for gems of information to answer your questions. Like all hunters, you will be active because you are searching for something. When you are more active, your understanding and memory will improve.

Okay, so now you've started seriously reading a chapter. What can you be doing to improve how effectively you read? Besides reading to answer your own questions, it's always a good idea to also **read to answer the question "What is the main idea?"**

Main ideas exist at different levels in a textbook. The main idea of this workbook, for example, is that students can learn to study more effectively. Each chapter within this workbook also contains a main idea. For instance, in this chapter the main ideas are that you can learn to improve how you study a textbook and improve your memory for things studied. Each section and paragraph within a chapter also contains a main idea. In the present section, the main idea is that SQ3R is a very effective learning strategy. The present paragraph's main idea is that main ideas exist at different levels within a book.

Another important goal of your reading should be to read for understanding. In most courses, memorization is unnecessary if you understand the material. Reading for the main idea of a paragraph will help your understanding. A good strategy is to **periodically interrupt your reading and monitor your understanding of what you have just read**. This practice is called "Self-Monitoring of Understanding" and it has been shown to be a powerful aid to study.

Get into the habit of self-monitoring your understanding during reading. Don't be afraid to pause to examine the meaning of an unfamiliar word. When you run across such a word, look at the context in which it occurs for clues to its meaning. If this fails, reach for your dictionary and look up the word. Repeat the meaning to yourself several times so you'll remember it. Now return to the sentence and reread it. Because you now know the meaning of all of the words, you will have a better understanding of the sentence.

It's also a good idea to stop briefly after every section and monitor your understanding of what you have just read. Many students who fail to do this self-monitoring waste hours reading only to realize at the end that they understood little of what they read. Continue reading if you understand what you read. Otherwise go back and reread the paragraph(s) and see if you can't get the main ideas.

Are there some things you shouldn't do during your first reading? It's probably *not* a good idea to try to make notes during the first reading. Making notes will be distracting and it will slow down your reading. When you make notes during an initial reading, there is also a tendency to use the author's words rather than your own. Taking notes in someone else's words won't help your understanding as much as using your own words.

Another thing you probably should not do during an initial reading is to underline in your text. On your first reading you may not recognize the most important ideas. If you underline during this reading, you often find that you've underlined the wrong things or minor points. There will be plenty of time later for underlining.

At this stage of the SQ3R learning method, many students find it very helpful to read the text twice. During their initial reading, they are concentrating on main ideas. On their second reading, these students self-monitor. They try to confirm that they were successful in picking out the main ideas. During the second reading they also pay more attention to supporting details and underline main ideas in each paragraph (if the book belongs to them).

In summary, these strategies can help improve the efficiency of your reading:

1. Precede your first reading with a survey.
2. Ask questions about what you will read.
3. Look for main ideas as you read.
4. Use periodic monitoring for understanding.
5. Don't underline or make notes during your first reading.
6. Reread. Check again for main ideas and also look for supporting details during your second reading. Underlining main ideas can be done during the second reading.

If you're interested in learning more about spotting the main ideas in a paragraph, go to Box 6 before you read the next SQ3R step.

Box 6

## Spotting the Main Idea in a Paragraph

Every paragraph generally has only one main idea. To understand what an author is trying to say in a paragraph requires that you be able to identify that main idea. Spotting the main idea of a paragraph becomes easier when you realize that there are different kinds of paragraphs. Each type of paragraph has a different purpose.

***Types of Paragraphs***

- **Information** paragraphs. These paragraphs give you information about a subject. The purpose of this type of paragraph is to provide information.
- **Proof** paragraphs. This type of paragraph tries to prove a point or to convince you of an idea. The purpose of a proof paragraph is to prove a point.
- **How-To** paragraphs. A How-To paragraph gives the reader a step-by-step description of how something is done. Its purpose is to give enough information so you could do the same thing yourself.
- **Definition** paragraphs. These paragraphs are designed to provide the definition of a phrase or word. The purpose of a definition paragraph is to help you learn the meaning of a term or concept.
- **Story** paragraphs. A story paragraph describes events which happened to someone. Its purpose is to tell a story.
- **Problem** paragraphs. A problem paragraph presents a problem and may also discuss its cause or solution. The purpose of a problem paragraph is to inform you of a problem and consider causes and solutions.

Learn to recognize the different types of paragraphs. When you know the type of paragraph, these questions can help you spot the main ideas.

***Spotting Main Ideas in a Paragraph***

- **Information** paragraphs. The topic is the main idea. Ask yourself what topic the information is about. Your answer to this question is the paragraph main idea.
- **Proof** paragraphs. Ask yourself what main point the author is trying to prove. The answer to this question is the main idea.
- **How-To** paragraphs. Ask yourself what the step-by-step procedure does or makes. The answer to this question will be the main idea of the paragraph.
- **Definition** paragraphs. Ask yourself what term or concept is being defined. The answer will be the main idea.
- **Story** paragraphs. Ask yourself what happened in the paragraph. The answer will be the main idea.
- **Problem** paragraphs. Ask yourself what problem or cause or solution is being discussed. The answer will be the main idea of the paragraph.

(Adapted from: Phipps, R. (1983). *The Successful Student's Handbook* Seattle: University of Washington Press.)

**Recite**

The fourth stage of the SQ3R learning strategy is to Recite what you have read. Reciting what you have read can be done in several ways. You may wish to include this Recite stage while you are reading. After a few paragraphs or a few pages, stop reading and recall by reciting to yourself what you have just read. In your own words, try to summarize the main ideas and see how the material answers your own questions. You may also wish to do the same sort of reciting at the end of a major section or chapter.

The reason for suggesting this frequent recitation or recall of what you have read is that it greatly improves memory. Without this type of active recitation, most people will forget half of what they read within a few seconds of closing a book.

The recitation stage of learning will help you study smarter. Not only will it help you remember things better, but it helps you concentrate because you know that you will later be "testing" yourself for recall. Frequent recitations also have a diagnostic purpose. They help you identify things you have forgotten or misunderstandings of what you've read. Lastly, recitation helps keep you active during learning. By reciting, you are putting main ideas into your own words. The process will help your understanding and memory.

How often should you recite during study? Look for your own happy medium. Reciting after every sentence is probably not necessary. It will break the text into too many small parts and make it disjointed. How about reciting after every paragraph? This might not be a bad idea if the paragraph is very long or very difficult. In most cases, it will probably be sufficient for you to recite at the end of a major section or subsection within the chapter. Try to get into the habit of stopping whenever you come to a new main heading. Pause and recite to yourself the main ideas of the prior section.

One last word about the value of recitation during learning. The students who obtain the most powerful benefits from recitation don't just think their recall. They write down the key points and main ideas they are recalling. Even if your recitation notes are very sketchy, they will be better than a half-formed thought which floats through your head. The danger is that you will become overconfident about how much you understood or remember. Writing down your recall and recitation will give you a much more accurate assessment of understanding and memory.

Some learning experts recommend that as much as half of your study time should be spent on active recitation or recall. How much time you spend on active recitation depends on the nature of the subject you are studying. Courses which include lots of material and concepts (such as economics, geography, history, language, etc.) should probably have a large recitation component in your study. Other courses which involve more application of material (such as mathematics, chemistry, computer science, etc.) should probably have somewhat less time spent on recitation with more time being spent on using what you have learned in solving problems or practice exercises.

In summary, you can use recitation or recall to improve your understanding and memory. Useful suggestions about the Recite stage include:

1. Develop the habit of reciting what you have learned during your study.
2. Use these recall breaks to remember the main ideas, review how the material answers your questions, and check the adequacy of your memory.
3. Don't just think during your recall. Write down what you are recalling and remembering in the form of short notes. Check back to see if you got it right and remember the main points.
4. Develop the habit of spending sizeable portions of your study time in active recitation.

**Review** The last step of SQ3R is to review what you have learned. An important purpose of the review stage is to double-check your understanding and memory of important material. All too often students assume that they "know the material" until they find out otherwise on a test. The Review stage of SQ3R allows you to check your mastery and memory while there is still time.

Many students find it useful to do a quick repeat of the first four steps of SQ3R during the review stage. They survey the chapter again and remind themselves of the questions they asked. Try to make time to reread the material again during the review. If there isn't time for this, at least review the important points you underlined or your notes. Complete your review by checking on the accuracy of your memory.

Another idea for review is to use review periods as self-quizzes. Several days or weeks after reading a chapter, go back to the questions you initially asked yourself about the chapter. See how many of them you can still answer. Be sure to check your answers for accuracy. If you don't do so well on your review quiz, you'll still have time to brush up your understanding and memory before you have to face the real examination.

**The Value of SQ3R** SQ3R study methods have been successfully used by thousands of students like yourself. Studies have shown that the method yields better understanding and memory than the way most students study. The proven success of SQ3R rests on the fact that you become more actively involved in learning when you use this approach.

Don't think of SQ3R as rigid. You can bend and adapt it to best suit your own individual learning style. Give it a try. You'll be pleased with the results.

Perhaps the biggest hesitation that students have about using the SQ3R approach is the fear that it will be too time consuming. Actually, research has shown the exact opposite! Students who use SQ3R read and learn faster than students who don't use the method. Why? When you read to answer questions, your attention and concentration improves and study efficiency improves as a result. The recitation and review components of SQ3R ensure that the information you read is stored in memory and that you will be able to remember it. These benefits combine to make SQ3R more time efficient than other less active study methods.

SQ3R is not a magic shortcut. You will still have to become involved, read the material, understand it, and remember it. The trick to "studying smarter" is to study more efficiently. Efficient study maximizes your attention, concentration, understanding, and memory. Give SQ3R a try. Use it for a few weeks in at least one of your courses and see if you don't notice a difference.

☞ go to **2**

**2**

"Memory is the receptacle and sheath of all knowledge."

*Cicero*

Success as a student depends heavily upon the adequacy of your memory. As implied in Cicero's quotation, what you have learned in your studies won't do you much good if you can't remember it. Answer the following checklist to see if you could benefit from efforts to improve your memory.

| Yes | No | |
|---|---|---|
| ❑ | ❑ | 1. When I watch TV reruns, they seem new to me. (Just kidding!) |
| ❑ | ❑ | 2. I often wish my memory for things I have studied was better. |
| ❑ | ❑ | 3. I am interested in learning new strategies to improve my memory. |
| ❑ | ❑ | 4. I often try to memorize something rather than using my own words to remember it. |
| ❑ | ❑ | 5. I often do poorly in courses that require a lot of memorization. |
| ❑ | ❑ | 6. I feel I would do better in my courses if I had a better memory. |

If you answered "No" to each of these items, you either have the memory of an elephant or have forgotten what your memory is really like. Feel free to scan section **3** to see if any of the memory enhancement strategies might be of interest. Otherwise, go to **6**.

If you answered "Yes" to one or more of the items, you are more like the rest of us. Who among us hasn't wished at one time or other for a better memory? To discover some strategies to improve your memory, go to **3**.

**3**

## Improving Your Memory

Many students use a "poor memory" as an excuse for doing badly in coursework. Studies show, however, that most people have remarkably similar memory capabilities. When memory appears to be worse in some students, it is usually because these students have not learned material as well as students who seem to have a "better" memory. In short, your memory is really a test of how well you've learned material in the first place!

Judging from how rapidly most students forget what they read, there is considerable room for improvement in initial learning. In fact, the figures are downright depressing! When we casually read something, about 50% of the material is forgotten in minutes. Nearly 75% of the material is forgotten after one week and about 95% is lost within four weeks. Clearly a successful student can't afford this much forgetting!

Read on to see how you can use the "M I N D" strategy to help improve your memory. "M I N D" looks like this:

| | |
|---|---|
| **M** | **Manage** effective study |
| **I** | **Intend** to remember |
| **N** | **Nudge** memory with mnemonics |
| **D** | **Do** something with the material |

**Manage effective study**
Most of you probably read about the SQ3R study method earlier in this chapter. One of the great fringe benefits of this study method is that it not only increases your mastery of what you read, but it also improves your retention. I don't want this to sound like a commercial, but the best way to improve your memory is really to manage more effective study. A SQ3R-like approach is one of the best ways to become a more active and effective learner.

Give it a try. I think you'll be pleasantly surprised at the results. Because the SQ3R study strategy helps you learn better, it automatically increases your memory for things you have learned. When you learn more effectively, remembering will become more natural and lasting.

**Intend to remember**
The first step in remembering something requires that you actually perceive whatever it is that is to be remembered. Information which was never taken in and perceived will not be remembered. This stage of memory is sometimes referred to as "Reception."

A good example of memory failure which occurs because of Reception difficulties is the ease with which people forget the names of newly introduced persons. How often have you been introduced to someone only to find that you have "forgotten" their name a few minutes later? Actually, in most cases our memories fail us in these situations because we never really listened closely enough during the introductions to actually register the name. We are usually a little nervous when meeting others for the first time and this nervousness can prevent us from even hearing the names.

Students sometimes find themselves in a similar situation with their studies. After reading an assignment they find that they remember very little. All too often, the problem is that the student casually read the assignment and hoped that it would "stick." Unfortunately memory doesn't work this way. To remember something, you must first select and perceive the information you wish to remember. In other words, the first step in remembering is to make a conscious decision that you want to remember something. Once you **intend to remember**, follow through on your good intention by using the last two steps of M I N D.

**Nudge memory with mnemonics**
Time for a little experiment.
Look at these two lists of letters.

| *List 1* | *List 2* |
|---|---|
| chair | xnpfm |
| home | nfqd |
| car | pvx |
| pencil | tyvxqp |
| horn | cqrm |

Now cover the two lists with a sheet of paper. Once you have the lists covered, look away from this page and think of something else for about 60 seconds.

When you return, keep the lists covered and without looking at them, write down as many of the items from each list as you can remember. How did you do? The chances are good that you remembered most or all of the items from List 1 and few or none of the items from List 2.

You may have already guessed the reason behind the differences in your memory for the two lists. You're right if you guessed that you remembered more items from List 1 because all these items were familiar words. The unfamiliar "nonsense words" of List 2 are much more difficult to remember because they are meaningless. It is much easier to remember meaningful material than material having little personal meaning.

We'll say more about this important principle of memory later in the last step of M I N D. For now, the above experiment has an important implication for improving your own memory. The results of the experiment suggest that **memory can be improved by making the to-be-remembered material more meaningful.**

Reading for understanding is the first step in trying to make material more meaningful. When you understand something you have read, you are able to express it in your own words and relate it to your own experience. Relating material to your own experience is especially helpful in making the information more meaningful. A few minutes spent during review thinking about how the information relates to you will greatly aid memory.

Unfortunately, not all of the course material you are expected to learn and remember is meaningful. The fact is that students are expected to remember lists, to memorize things, and to know facts which may have little personal meaningfulness. One way to "create meaning where there is none" is to use a memory trick called a mnemonic.

A mnemonic (pronounced "ni-mon-ic") is a strategy designed to assist memory. Mnemonics help you remember material by relating it to something more meaningful. When you use a mnemonic, you make the to-be-remembered material more meaningful and thereby easier to remember.

Mnemonics are especially useful for remembering lists of information. **The two most common types of mnemonics are "Initial Letters" and "Locations."** Both methods use a strategy which attaches bits of information to a meaningful "hook" which is easier to remember.

**The method of Initial Letters**

Suppose you are faced with remembering a list of key words. In the method of initial letters, you try to form the key words into a single word or sentence. That word or sentence then reminds you of each key word.

The method of Initial Letters has been frequently used in this workbook. In this chapter, for example, the "M I N D" strategy represents an initial letter mnemonic. Each letter of MIND corresponds to a key strategy for improving memory.

Some mnemonic sentences are very common and are actually taught as part of a course. Have you ever had to learn the names and correct order of the 12 cranial nerves, for example? It's a real struggle to remember the list "Olfactory, Optic, Oculomotor, Trochlear,Trigeminal, Abducens, Facial, Auditory, Glossopharyngeal, Vagus, Spinal, and Hypoglossal" using brute memorization. The task becomes considerably easier after your biology teacher introduces you to the well known mnemonic "On Old Olympus Towering Top, A Finn And German Viewed Some Hops." Using this mnemonic sentence, the first letter of each word corresponds to the first letter of the corresponding facial nerve.

Another well known example of sentence and word mnemonics is used to remember the letters of the musical staff. It's much easier to recall the letters of the staff when you use the memory hooks: "Every Good Boy Does Fine" and "FACE." The first letters of the sentence correspond to the names of notes on the treble staff lines while FACE represents the note names for the spaces on the treble staff.

Consider another example of a sentence mnemonic. For years, I've had difficulty remembering the order of the planets in the solar system (starting from the sun: Mercury, Venus, Earth, Mars, Jupiter, Saturn, Uranus, Neptune, and Pluto). Recently, I was introduced to the sentence mnemonic "My Very Excellent Mother Just Served Us Nine Pickles." Remembering this sentence proved remarkably easy. Now when I want to recall the order of the planets, I simply remember this sentence and use the first letters of each word to identify the appropriate planet and its order.

The next time you're faced with memorizing a list, try using your own "custom designed" sentence or word mnemonic. It beats relying on rote memorization!

**The method of Locations**

This mnemonic involves "putting" the items to be remembered in a familiar location. Later, when you remember the location, you'll remember the item you "put" in that location.

You might use each room of your house as the familiar location. Imagine coming in the front door. Put the first item on your list in the front hall. Now mentally move to the living room and deposit another item on your list in the living room and so on until you've mentally deposited all of the items in various rooms of your house. As you "deposit" an item, form a mental image of the item in it's mental location. (The method of locations works even better if you visualize something really strange or funny at each step.)

Suppose that you want to remember a list of grocery items. Let's say that your list contains these items: eggs, apples, bread, garbage bags, tooth paste, and laundry soap. Now mentally associate each item to a room in your house. You might visualize yourself standing in the front hall balancing an egg on your head. Moving into the living room, you mentally see an apple attached to a wall with an arrow sticking through it. As you mentally enter the kitchen, you notice the delicious smell of bread coming from the oven and glance over to see that the garbage pail is overflowing. Entering the bathroom you visualize an empty tube of toothpaste on the counter. In the laundry room you form the mental image of massive amounts of suds coming out of the washing machine. (The more outlandish your mental images, the better you'll remember them.)

After you've made your mental list of locations, you simply retrace your steps to remember the items associated with each location. The method of locations can also be used to remember lists of information from your courses. Can you think of any lists from your coursework which could be remembered using this mnemonic?

**Do something with the material**

The last step in the M I N D memory strategy is to do something with the material. Actively processing the information will help you store it in memory and improve later recall. The following strategies can be used to actively process information and increase memory:

**Organize the information**. Process what you are learning by organizing and personalizing the information. For example, making outlines of key points will help you organize and remember the information. Information which is well organized is much easier to remember than a random list of ideas. Try to make your organization personal and individual.

**Link the material with existing knowledge.** Simply thinking about new information and relating it to what you already know will help your memory. This type of active processing is a valuable help to memory. It helps make the information more meaningful. It helps increase understanding. It will also help later recall because it "files" the new information in your memory along with related memories.

**Look for examples and applications.** This keeps you actively processing the information and makes it more likely that you will remember it. Suppose, for example, that you are learning about enzyme reactions in a biochemistry course. You have studied the meaning of enzymes and have studied the characteristics of enzyme reactions. To make this material more memorable, look for examples of how this knowledge might be applied. How might manufacturers use enzymes in making laundry detergents? (Maybe an enzyme to help break down perspiration stains?) Would enzymes be helpful in dissolving blood clots? What conditions would be necessary to help use enzymes to treat sewage? These are just a few examples of how looking for examples and applications for the concept of "enzyme" can aid your study and memory.

Coming up with examples and applications helps make the material more personally interesting and it helps link the material with existing knowledge. It tries out your new knowledge on examples and new applications. It keeps you actively processing the knowledge so you will remember it. Who knows. Maybe you'll come up with a new application that will make you rich (as well as wise).

**Analyse and Evaluate information.** Analysing and evaluating new information keeps you thinking. Besides helping develop the thinking skills necessary for success in school, it will help your memory.

**Find the underlying principle.** Rather than trying to just memorize facts, look for the underlying principle. Principles and concepts are much easier to remember than figures and facts.

**Reinforce memory with repetition.** The best known way to increase memory is to repeat the material over and over. This repetition helps your brain transfer the information from temporary storage to long term memory. Failure to repeat information enough times is probably the single greatest cause of poor memory. Students often read something once and are distressed when they can't remember it.

Remember the last part of SQ3R? This "Review" stage is designed to provide the repetition necessary for good memory. Please don't underestimate the power of repetition and review in your studies. Review is critically important for memory. When you plan your study time, be sure to include regular review sessions.

Another example of the use of repetition to aid memory is to use the material frequently. This strategy is especially helpful in remembering science or math formulas. By using the formula on many different problems or equations, you'll be more likely to remember it.

☞ go to **5**

## 4

It's time for a change! Take a short break if you need one. When you come back (or continue), practice using SQ3R in one of your courses while what you have just read is still fresh in your mind.

Pick one of your courses. Arrange for an hour (or more) of study in this course and use SQ3R. Use this summary checklist to guide your study:

☐ **Survey** the material. Page through the material you plan to read during the study session. Look at the chapter title, headings, and subheadings. Notice any illustrations and read the captions. Read any summaries or learning goals.

☐ **Question** yourself. Write down specific questions about what you will read. Use your survey to suggest questions.

☐ **Read** the material. Read to find the answers to your questions. Try to identify the main points during your reading.

Re-read the material. Check to see that you have spotted the answers to your questions and have identified main points. Look for supporting details and information during your second reading.

☐ Recite what you have learned. Review to yourself what you have just learned. Put it into your own words. Relate it to your personal experience. Link it with what you already know. Think of other examples. Try to make the material more meaningful. Check how accurately you have remembered the material.

☐ **Review** the material. Save a few minutes of the study session for a final quick review. Schedule some time later to do a more thorough review.

At first, using SQ3R may not come naturally. It requires more active involvement in study than most students are used to. Keep at it and you'll find that "practice makes perfect." For example, with practice you'll start to automatically ask questions at the same time that you do your survey. With practice, you will also automatically read to find the answers to your questions and to identify the main points. Practice also reinforces reciting, recalling, and review. Together they'll make a big contribution to "studying smarter."

After you've tried SQ3R, you can return to this workbook to pick up additional survival strategies. When you return,

☞ go to **2**

## 5

"M I N D" helped organize a number of proven strategies for improving memory. Like any of the strategies in this workbook, they won't do you much good unless you start using some of them in your own studies.

Spend a few minutes now thinking about some of the memory improvement strategies of M I N D which seem most relevant to your own individual learning style and habits. Make an informal contract with yourself about strategies you plan to start using in your studies. Use this space to make a note of what strategies you plan to start using.

**M** *Managing effective study* I plan to:

------------------------------------------------

------------------------------------------------

------------------------------------------------

------------------------------------------------

------------------------------------------------

------------------------------------------------

------------------------------------------------

------------------------------------------------

------------------------------------------------

------------------------------------------------

**I** *Intend to remember* I plan to:

**N** *Nudge memory with mnemonics* I will make use of:

**D** *Do something with the material* To more actively process information, I will:

Once you have established your memory improvement goals, begin to apply them during your studies. Come back here every now and then to refresh your memory. In short, try to develop the habit of routinely using your memory enhancement strategies. Before you know it, they'll become a normal part of your everyday studying.

☞ go to **6**

**6**

This chapter has shared some powerful and proven strategies for improving the efficiency of your study and memory. It might not seem so now, but these strategies will be real time savers. They will save you from wasting valuable study time and will let you get much more out of your present study time. Good luck in your efforts to use them to "study smarter, not harder."

When you're ready (perhaps later or after a break), come back and have a look at another chapter which seems most interesting.

"YOU SIMPLY ASSOCIATE EACH NUMBER WITH A WORD, SUCH AS 'TABLE' AND 3,476,029."

# CHAPTER 5
# Listening and Notetaking

**In this chapter you can learn**

- *how to improve listening during class*
- *how to take more useful class notes*

This chapter contains tips for improving how much you get out of your attendance at classes. It will help improve your classroom listening skills and share strategies for improving the usefulness of class notes. To see if you could benefit from these strategies, take the following check.

| Yes | No | |
|---|---|---|
| ❑ | ❑ | 1. I am easily distracted during a lecture. |
| ❑ | ❑ | 2. There are frequent periods during a lecture when I can't remember what was said. |
| ❑ | ❑ | 3. I often daydream during class. |
| | | 4. I am often bored during a lecture. |
| ❑ | ❑ | 5. When I disagree with what is being said, I stop listening. |
| ❑ | ❑ | 6. I frequently miss hearing key concepts or important terms during a lecture. |

If you answered "Yes" to some of these items, you could probably benefit from learning how to become a more effective listener.

☞ go to **1**

If you answered "No" to each of the items, your classroom listening habits are probably already adequate. If you're interested in briefly scanning for new tips on listening, go to **1** . Otherwise,

☞ go to **2**

**1**

## Becoming a More Effective Listener

"A good listener is not only popular everywhere, but after a while he (or she) knows something."
*Wilson Mizner*

To get the most out of your classes, it is important to develop good listening habits. Surprisingly, listening is not as easy or natural as you might imagine. We tend to listen in short spurts. After a few seconds of listening, our attention wanders away for a short time and then returns. Usually we are not even aware that this is happening.

How well we listen is influenced by many factors. For example, we all tend to tune out things we do not really want to hear. What we do hear is influenced by our expectations, our prejudices, our past experiences, and our beliefs. We're more likely to hear information that corresponds to our beliefs than something which contradicts them. We also tend to listen poorly when we are doing something else. Our listening tends to be best when we have a purpose for listening. With a purpose, we tend to hear more and better because our listening is actively searching for information to satisfy our purpose.

Although we all have received extensive training in reading and writing, no one teaches students much about listening. Yet listening is one of the important ways in which we learn. This section will share some ideas on effective listening. By learning to listen more effectively, you'll find that you get more out of your classes and that your class notes become more effective learning aids.

### Strategies to Improve Classroom Listening

I've used the mnemonic "H E A R" to help you remember some strategies for improving classroom listening. The components of the H E A R model are:

H Get a **Head start**

E **Engage** yourself

A **Absorb** yourself

R **React** to signals

### Get a Head Start

The first step for improving the efficiency of classroom listening is to get a head start. Getting a head start involves preparing for the lecture. Some things you can do to prepare include:

•**Know the purpose of the lecture.** What topics will be covered? Your course outline will give information. Many instructors start out a lecture by giving an overview of what topics will be covered. Pay special attention at the beginning of every lecture to see if your teacher does this. It's also a good idea to review your notes from the last class. This will refresh your memory about what was covered last.

• **Get ready to listen.** Become familiar with the material which will be covered in the lecture. Read assigned materials before coming to class. If the instructor follows the assigned materials closely during lectures, you'll have a head start by reading assignments before class.

• **Try to anticipate what the teacher will say next.** Reading assignments before they are discussed in class will help you anticipate what the teacher is going to say in class. During a class, try to guess what your instructor is going to say next. This can be an interesting little game which helps keep you alert even if the lecture is badly delivered.

• **Ask questions.** Ask yourself questions about what might be covered during the lecture. Using your reading and opening comments from the teacher, pose questions and then listen for the answers.

• **Get a good seat.** If possible, come to class a few minutes early so that you have a few minutes to get your "head start." The best seats in the house are up-front. Besides not having to use binoculars, you'll also be able to hear the lecture better.

**Engage Yourself**

This step of H E A R recommends that you engage yourself to become a more active listener. We usually think of listening as a passive process. Someone else is producing the words and we are passively absorbing them. Effective listening is not passive. You'll hear more of what is said in class if you become an active, engaged listener. Here are some ways to become more active during listening.

• **Listen for the purpose of the lecture.** Learn to identify what each teacher does during lectures. Also be alert to the purpose served by different parts of the same lecture. If you can identify the purpose of the lecture (or each part of it), you'll be in a better position to know what to listen for.

Identifying the purpose of a lecture (or different parts of it) may be a little easier if you look at what teachers usually do in class. Teachers typically organize lectures to reflect a few general goals. Common lecture goals include:

1) Lectures designed to present new information which is not included in the assigned readings.
2) Lectures designed to offer more explanations for difficult ideas or concepts.
3) Lectures intended to explain and give practice for new skills.
4) Lectures consisting of demonstrations (as in chemistry or physics experiments).

When in class, listen carefully and decide which one of these things your teacher is doing at various class times. This judgment will help you decide how carefully you should be listening, whether you should be taking extensive notes, etc.

• **Listen for main ideas.** Another way to engage yourself and become a more active listener is to listen for main ideas. Many instructors will give special emphasis to major ideas by either repeating them or writing them on a chalkboard. Whenever an instructor writes something on the chalkboard or repeats, judge whether its a main idea. If so, make sure you listen especially well and try to get the main points down in your class notes.

• **Learn the lecture style of the teacher.** Most students soon become proficient in figuring out their teachers. In fact, learning about the lecturing style of your teachers can help learning. Look for a style or recurring pattern in lectures from the same teacher. Ask yourself questions such as "How much of this teacher's lecture usually covers material not found in the text or readings? Does the teacher start classes with a review? Does the teacher end classes by giving a summary of the lecture? Does the instructor use any special signals to indicate the importance of information?" Answers to these and similar questions can help you better know the individual teaching style of your teacher. This knowledge can improve your classroom listening.

• **Questions, questions, questions.** Don't forget to use self-questioning to engage yourself in listening. Fortunately, during most lectures you'll have plenty of time to pause for a few seconds after the teacher says something and think of a few quick mental questions. (You can think much faster than your teacher can talk.) Questions improve listening in much the same way that they work to improve study efficiency. By asking a question of yourself, you become more engaged in listening and your attention will be focused to actively listen for answers.

In addition to self-questions, don't be reluctant to ask questions of teachers during class. Most teachers welcome questions. When students ask questions, it indicates that they are active, involved, and interested (as well as awake). When a teacher presents something in class you don't understand, don't be hesitant to ask for clarification.

• **Respond to the teacher.** Another strategy for engaging yourself as an active listener is to respond to the teacher. When you aren't taking notes, look at the teacher. If you agree with what is being said, nod your head. If you disagree or don't understand, frown or shake your head. Laugh at the jokes. Look alive. Teachers thrive on alert and responsive classes. A good teacher becomes even better when students show that they are attentive and interested.

**Absorb yourself in the lecture**

The third part of H E A R is to become a better listener by absorbing yourself in what is being said. Concentration is essential for effective listening. If you are bored or easily distracted during class, your listening will suffer. You end up getting little out of class. It certainly makes sense to make more efficient use of class time by trying to improve your concentration and listening.

Here are some strategies that other students have found helpful.

• **Take notes.** Don't just sit there waiting for the next joke. Listen for something important and write it down in your notes. Taking notes keeps you active and helps you concentrate on what is being said.

• **Focus on the class.** Be alert to those times when your mind will naturally wander. Develop the habit of periodically monitoring your attention. Were you thinking about something other than what the teacher was saying? If so, refocus your attention on the class.

Some students who have difficulty concentrating during class find it helpful to make a check mark every time they find themselves not concentrating on what is being said. Initially they may have 20 or 30 checkmarks during a lecture, but after a week or two of trying to improve their concentration they are often able to reduce the number of checks to one or two per lecture.

• **Don't be distracted by teacher mannerisms.** We've all probably had a teacher who says "you know" or "ah" 200 times a lecture. This, or similar distracting mannerisms, can keep you from concentrating on what is being said. If you have a teacher with distracting mannerisms, learn to ignore these personal quirks and concentrate on what is being said.

• **Maintain eye contact with the speaker.** Maintaining eye contact with a speaker helps maintain our interest and concentration on what is being said.

• **Notice non-verbal messages.** Speakers typically communicate using non-verbal as well as verbal messages. "Listen" for non-verbal messages. Further absorb yourself in listening by attending to cues such as body posture, gestures, changes in speaking volume, and changes in speaking rate. Instructors often use these non-verbal messages to indicate the importance of material.

An example from my own lecture style as a professor comes to mind. Without actually consciously planning to do so, I've noticed that I pause and slow down to indicate when I'm presenting important material. Although I've never formally pointed this out to students in my classes, I've noticed that many of them learn to respond to this non-verbal cue by faithfully taking notes whenever I pause or slow down.

**React to Signals**

The last step of H E A R involves becoming a better listener by actively reacting to signals. Teachers use many different signals to indicate the importance of material. You can become a more effective listener by learning to spot and use these cues. Some ways to use these cues for more effective listening are presented here.

• Listen for the obvious. Many teachers are straightforward in telling students when something is important or will be on a test. Only a foolhardy or apathetic student neglects listening or notetaking when an instructor says something like "This is important." or "Keep this in mind for the test." or "It's important to remember that..."

Another "obvious" technique used by many teachers to highlight central or important material is repetition. As a general rule, if the teacher repeats something more than once it's important. Get it down in your notes and make sure you hear what is said.

Many teachers use the chalkboard to highlight important concepts or terms. As a general rule, if the teacher thinks it's important enough to be on the chalkboard, it's probably important enough to be in your notes. React similarly to anything the teacher writes on an overhead or shows on a transparency.

• **Listen for clues about key ideas.** Listen for these key words in a lecture:
**basic...important...significant...central...focus...**
**first...second...critical...**
**the reasons for...in conclusion...**
**remember that...finally...most importantly...**
**a major finding...the basic idea is...**

Instructors commonly use these words to signify that key points will follow. Whenever you hear these clues, "put on your ears" and become an active listener and notetaker.

• **Listen for clues about supporting information.** These words often indicate that the teacher will be presenting material to support main ideas:
**also...for example...an example of...**
**on the other hand...similarly...further...**
**furthermore...contrary to**
Listen for these words in a lecture and use them to signal that supporting details are likely to follow.

• **Listen for instructions.** Become especially attentive whenever the teacher talks about course assignments or upcoming examinations. Listen for all the details and requirements. Teachers will often give you a good idea of the relative weight that will be given to various topics on exams. Use this information to study appropriately.

**Using H E A R to become a better listener**
Go to the head of the class if you've noticed that every H E A R strategy recommends becoming more active during listening. Like learning, listening will be improved if you strive to make it a more active process.

Some of the key ways you can use H E A R to become a more effective listener are summarized here:

**H** Get a **Head start**
• Know the purpose of a lecture beforehand. Review notes from last class.
• Ask yourself questions about what is likely to be covered in the class.
• Get ready to listen. Forget about other concerns and concentrate on the class.
• Anticipate what the teacher might say next and listen for it.

**E Engage** yourself
• Listen for the purpose of the lecture and each of its parts. Compare what you hear with what you thought you'd hear.
• Listen for the main ideas.
• Learn the teacher's lecture style and use what you learn to improve your listening skill.
• Ask questions to yourself during the class. Don't be afraid to ask questions of the teacher.
• Respond to the teacher.

**A Absorb** yourself
• Take notes during class.
• Focus your concentration on the class. Monitor your concentration during class.
• Ignore distracting teacher mannerisms.
• Notice non-verbal messages.

**R React** to signals
• Listen for obvious cues from the teacher.
• Listen for clues about key ideas.
• Listen for clues about supporting information
• Listen for instructions or study hints for tests.

☞ **go to 2**

**2**

The rest of this chapter explores strategies to improve notetaking skills. Answer the following checklist to see if you need to improve your own notetaking habits.

| Yes | No | |
|---|---|---|
| ❑ | ❑ | 1. My class notes are usually quite organized. |
| ❑ | ❑ | 2. I never try to write down every word the instructor says in my notes. (Mark "Yes" if this describes you. Mark "No" if you try to write down everything in your notes. |
| ❑ | ❑ | 3. I have a system of abbreviations I use to make class notes. |
| ❑ | ❑ | 4. I use a style of organization for all of my class notes. |
| ❑ | ❑ | 5. When I go back to read my notes, they usually make sense. |
| ❑ | ❑ | 6. I leave space on each page of notes to use for later comments and summaries. |
| ❑ | ❑ | 7. I usually use my class notes when reviewing for an exam. |
| ❑ | ❑ | 8. My notes are usually quite complete. |

If you can honestly answer "Yes" to all these items, you're an above-average notetaker. Read section **3** if you are interested in double checking possible ways to take even better notes. Otherwise,

☞ go to **4**

If you answered "No" to some of the items, you're more like the typical student. Note taking is difficult and most students could learn to take better and more useful notes. The notetaking strategies of section **3** will probably be helpful to you.

☞ go to **3**

**3**

## Making Your Notes Work For You

If you've studied section **1** of this chapter, you're already on your way to taking better notes. The effective listening strategies of section 1 lay the foundation for taking more useful notes. When you use these strategies, you come to class prepared and ready to spot main ideas and concepts. You're primed to be a better listener and notetaker.

The strategies for improving notetaking skills are organized using the mnemonic "W R I T E." The W R I T E model has five parts:

**W** **Why** you take notes

**R** **Routinely** organize your notes

**I** **Ignore** unnecessary material

**T** **Tally** the main ideas

**E** **Engage** in review

**Why you take notes**
Unless you're really convinced that notetaking is helpful, you won't have much desire to improve your present notetaking skills. To get you thinking about what notes can do for you, consider some things that other students find useful about a good set of notes.

- An organized set of notes helps identify the important ideas in lectures.
- Good notes give a permanent record which will help learning and memory.
- Some lectures contain information not available elsewhere. Your notes will be your only record. You'll have to learn this material directly from your notes.
- Instructors generally spend valuable class time on the most important information. Looking over notes helps you decide what is most important when preparing for exams.
- Notes provide a record of assignments given in lectures.
- Notes can help you see the way lectures are organized and their purpose.
- Taking notes helps maintain your concentration (especially if the lecture is not too exciting).
- Taking notes helps prevent your mind from wandering during lectures.

In short, well organized notes can be an important help for better learning. If you keep this in mind for every class, you'll be much more interested in making and using notes for your best advantage.

**Routinely Organize Your Notes**

The second step of W R I T E is to discover a routine way to organize your notes. One of the biggest problems students report about class notes is that they end up being disorganized to the point where they offer little help for later review.

There is no one method of organizing notes which is "best." The strategies presented here have worked for many students. Have a look at them and decide which ones might be most helpful to you.

• **Use loose sheets of paper kept in a binder.** Using loose sheets of paper stored in a ring binder is preferred by many good students. (It beats making notes on scraps of paper or on the back of envelopes!). The advantage of using loose sheets of paper is that you can add sheets easily. For example, you might wish to add some summary notes from your textbook. These can be easily inserted into your binder at the appropriate spot. When you use an already bound notebook, you are forced to store your notes in the order in which you write them.

• **Put identifying information on notepaper before class.** Put your name and the course name at the top of each sheet. Also enter the date of the current lecture. It's a good idea to number each page. If this information is on each page, at least you have a chance of getting your notes back and in order if they are misplaced or the pages become mixed up. Do this before class so you don't have to waste class time on it.

• **Write on one side of the paper.** This can come in handy when you are reviewing your notes. By spreading them out, you can see all of them at the same time.

• **Leave space on each page for notes and comments.** One highly recommended approach is to take each page you'll use for notes and draw a vertical line about 7 cm from the left side of the page. (Do this *before* coming to class.) Use the space on the right side of the page for class notes. The space on the left can be used for comments, additional information, summaries, outlines, etc. (more on this later).

• **Develop a routine system for marking main topics.** You might try putting main topics flush with the vertical line on the left and indenting subtopics. Some students draw a box around a main topic heading. Others simply underline a main topic. Perhaps you prefer to just number main topics. Use whatever works best but be consistent. The big ideas should stand out like traffic lights! That way, when you return to study your notes you'll always be able to immediately spot every main topic.

• **Try to write legibly.** You don't have to be a neatness freak, but do write carefully enough so you'll be able to read your own writing later.

• **Take notes in your own words.** Unless you are recording precise technical terms, it is better to take your notes in your own words rather than merely transcribing the words of the instructor. It will help you understand the information better.

### Ignore Unnecessary Material

A common trap for students is to try to write down everything the instructor says in class. This is an exercise in frustration. Unless you are an expert in taking shorthand, it's impossible to write as fast as someone can talk.

You may not believe it, but I've actually had students approach me after a lecture to ask me to repeat one word out of a sentence. This has happened so frequently that I found myself doing two things. First, I would look at the immediate context of the students notes to see what general area I was talking about and then summarize the main idea for the student. Secondly, I gently suggested that students concentrate on getting main ideas in their notes rather than a verbatim transcript of everything I said.

The following strategies may help you concentrate on getting better notes by ignoring unnecessary material:

• **Don't make notes on an initial review.** Many instructors will begin each class by making a brief review of the previous lecture. Listen to the review, but don't bother writing it down in your notes (unless you missed it before).

• **Rest your hand during digressions.** Learn to spot when your instructor goes off on a tangent. There is no need to make notes on these digressions. I can think of only one exception to this rule. Some students think that questions from other students are digressions. When the instructor is answering these questions, the pens often go down and everyone relaxes. Actually, my own experience indicates that most student questions are directly relevant to topics under discussion. Like many other instructors, I often take the opportunity of answering a question to bring in more material or emphasize certain points.

• **Write down only key words and phrases.** Don't try to write down everything the instructor says. Instead, concentrate on the key elements. Leave out unnecessary adjectives or articles (e.g. a, an, the).

• **Use a system of abbreviations for common words and terms.** Develop your own system or use other common abbreviations such as those presented in Box 7. One form of speed writing leaves out the vowels. Cn u rd ths? Be careful in leaving out too much—you want to be able to read it when you look at it later. The selective use of abbreviations such as those in Box 7 can, however, be very helpful in taking notes from lectures.

Box 7

**Tips for Using Abbreviations in Lecture Notes**

During lectures, you should be listening more than you write. Here are some abbreviations and tips to help you write faster.

| | |
|---|---|
| **ex = example** | **lk = like** |
| **b/c = because** | **b/4 = before** |
| **p. = page** | **no. or # = number** |
| **wd = word** | **ref = reference** |
| **wrt = write** | **rt = right** |
| **i.e. = that is** | **etc. = and so on** |
| **\ = therefore** | **vs = versus or as opposed to** |
| **ch = chapter** | **2 = to, too, two** |
| **w/ = with** | **w/o = without** |
| **diff = different** | **lrn = learn** |
| **Q = question** | **gvt = government** |
| **rctn = reaction** | **dept = department** |
| **markg = marking** | **= = equals** |
| **< = less than** | **> = greater than** |
| **nb = note well** | **& = and** |
| **xs = excess** | **abbv = abbreviated** |

If you're in a hurry, don't bother crossing your t's and dotting your i's. Shorten long words by omitting the vowels. Use dashes for words when the teacher goes too fast. Leave space so that you can come back and fill in the details later. Don't bother erasing mistakes. Just draw a single line through it.

**Tally the Main Ideas**

At this point in the W R I T E model, you're ready to start using your notes. The most complete and accurate set of notes won't do you much good if you don't use them. After class, it's time to come back to your notes and "tally the main ideas."

Remember that unused left column we suggested you leave on each page of your notes? This is the place where you can now start tallying the main ideas of the notes. The word "tally" is being used in a general sense to suggest that you should **actively do something with your notes.** Here are some strategies which can help your notes become more powerful learning aids:

- **Fill in gaps and unintelligible parts.** As soon as you can after class, have a look at your notes while your memory is still fresh. Start by filling in any missing parts. Can you read everything? If not, rewrite anything you can't read while you still remember what it is. Write out any abbreviations you may not recognize later.

- **Add comments to make notes clearer.** Use your initial pass through your notes right after class to make them clearer. Add comments on the left side which clarify ideas. Fill in any missing details. Underline or mark major ideas or concepts.

- **Write key phrases and words on the left side.** Do this as soon after the lecture as possible. The longer you wait, the more of the lecture you'll have forgotten. The process of writing the key words and phrases on the left side of your notes will help you remember the lecture and help fix the information in your memory.

- **Use the key words to help you recall the lecture.** Once you've written the key words on the left side of the page, an excellent learning strategy is to cover the right hand side and see if you can recall the meaning of the key words. Try to use your own words to describe the meaning of the key words. Then uncover the notes and check the accuracy of your recall.

- **Think about the meaning of the lecture.** Can you think of examples from your own knowledge or experience which illustrate any of the lecture points? This reflection stage of reviewing your notes can be one of the most powerful stages of the learning process. It is during this stage that you are integrating the information.

As we've seen earlier, relating new information to what you already know is a powerful strategy for increasing both understanding and memory.

"GOT IDEA. TALK BETTER. COMBINE WORDS. MAKE SENTENCES."

Make time for this stage of W R I T E. It only takes a few minutes and it can make the difference between having notes which are a valuable help to learning versus notes which are worthless. The majority of below-average students fail to make adequate use of their notes. Their notes are often disorganized and they never use them until right before an exam. This habit is generally one of the reasons these students are below average.

**Engage in Review**

The last stage of the W R I T E model recommends periodic review and reflection. The same types of recitation and review which form such important parts of SQ3R can be applied to reviewing your notes.

Reserve a portion of your regularly scheduled review time to review your notes. Take out your notes and lay them out so that only the key words on the left are showing. Using these key words as cues, remember as much as possible about the ideas and information presented in each lecture. The more frequently you do this, the better you'll remember the material.

☞ go to 4

**4**

At this point you've read about either the H E A R strategies for improved listening or the W R I T E strategies for improved notetaking (or both of them). Space limitations prevent including practice exercises for these strategies. Why not design your own "real life" practice exercise? Decide which strategies you want to try and start using them on one or more of your courses.

The H E A R strategies for better listening are the easiest. They don't require any extra work on your part but by using them you'll automatically get more out of your classes. The W R I T E strategies for better notes do require some extra work. Most students aren't used to going back to their notes and organizing them for a periodic review. However, the experience of many students like yourself has been that this little extra work is well worth the effort in helping you to study smarter, not harder.

Time now for a break. When you're ready, come back and look at the next chapter or another one that looks useful.

"YES, I AGREE THAT MAN IS MASTER OF HIS OWN DESTINY, BUT SOMETIMES IT HELPS IF YOU PASS ALGEBRA."

# CHAPTER 6
# Solving Problems in Math and Science

**In this chapter you can learn**

- *how to study math and science courses*
- *how to tackle math and science problems*

Many students find courses in mathematics and the physical sciences more difficult than their other coursework. In a recent survey of students, math and science courses were reported as being most difficult and students placed a high priority on improving problem-solving skills in these courses.

Chapter 6 presents strategies for improving study efficiency in math and science courses. The chapter also introduces strategies which can improve problem solving skills in these courses. To see if you could benefit from of Chapter 6, please answer the following checklist.

| Yes | No | |
|---|---|---|
| ☐ | ☐ | 1. I find math and science courses more difficult than many of my other courses. |
| ☐ | ☐ | 2. I often have difficulties solving practice problems in math or science courses. |
| ☐ | ☐ | 3. I sometimes spend long periods of time trying to solve a single difficult problem. |
| ☐ | ☐ | 4. I often skip difficult paragraphs in a math or science textbook. |
| ☐ | ☐ | 5. In a math or science textbook I often skip paragraphs with equations. |
| ☐ | ☐ | 6. I often rely on sheer memorization to get through a math or science course. |

If you answered "No" to each of these items, you are probably already a "whiz" in your math and science courses and solving practice problems in these courses isn't especially difficult for you. If this sounds like you, it's probably okay to skip the rest of this chapter. Feel free to make a quick scan first, just to make sure that you don't miss any tips which could be useful.

If you answered "Yes" to some of the items, you'll probably benefit by giving the rest of this chapter careful attention.

☞ go to **1**

**1**

## Study Strategies for Math and Science Courses

All of the learning strategies presented in previous chapters of this workbook are applicable to math and science courses. For example, your study of math and science textbooks will be more efficient if you also apply the SQ3R study method to these courses. By surveying your math and science readings and asking questions, your study will be more effective. By recalling and reviewing, you'll have a better chance of remembering the important material.

The nature of math and science courses often differs from your other courses and the learning requirements are often different as well. In math courses, for example, the information is often perceived as more difficult by students. Added to this perception is the "phobia" that many students have about mathematics. Whenever they see a complex formula, many students experience a nasty feeling in the pit of their stomach, their eyes glaze over, and they quickly jump ahead to a section of the book that contains words rather than numbers or symbols.

Another way that math and science courses often differ from other courses is that the information is cumulative. That is, one unit of information builds on another. If you don't understand an early formula, you won't be able to grasp later information developed on the basis of a series of earlier steps. Other courses usually do not have this much of a cumulative nature.

One last difference between math and science courses versus other courses is worth mentioning. Your math and science courses often make greater demands on your memory. There are lots of facts, formulas, and details you're expected to remember. Many of these details seem unrelated to your experiences and you often find yourself relying more on brute memorization to retain them.

In short, your math and science courses do have some learning demands which are different from the demands of your other courses. When the learning demands of a course change, an efficient student makes the necessary changes in study habits to best meet the course demands.

The following section will introduce you to some special learning strategies which many students have found especially useful for math and science courses.

☞ go to **2**

**2**

**Tips for Studying Math and Science Texts**
When studying math and science courses, your learning efficiency will improve if you use the following strategies:

• **Use SQ3R to study.** Using the SQ3R study plan on math and science courses will help keep you actively involved in the learning process. Just as in other courses, your learning of math and science material will improve when you use SQ3R.

• **Read math and science texts differently.** Allow yourself more time for careful reading of math and science courses than you usually spend reading less difficult material. Don't be alarmed if you find yourself reading slower during math or science study. This is natural and even desirable when you are reading difficult material. The danger in reading math and/or science material is that you will read a difficult passage and continue on even though you haven't really understood something.

• **Ease the burden on your memory by using memory aids.** Science courses often have more material for brute memorization than other courses. Adding to the problem, much of this material may not seem applicable to your own experience. When dealing with this type of material, it will be especially helpful to use all of the memory aids discussed in Chapter 4. For example, in math and science courses always try to really understand the material. Material which is understood is much easier to recall than information which was simply memorized. Also try to always relate the material to your past experience or think of new examples. This active processing also improves memory. Lastly, mathematics and science courses offer excellent opportunities for the use of mnemonic aids. Get into the habit of devising your own mnemonics to help you remember material which must be memorized.

• **Monitor frequently for understanding.** When material is complicated or difficult, it is especially important to self-monitor for understanding during reading. In a course you find easier, it may be quite sufficient to monitor for self-understanding (a strategy first discussed in Chapter 4) less frequently. Stopping and checking for understanding after every main section will probably be quite adequate in these courses. This is not the case when you are trying to comprehend more difficult material. If you fail to understand the first several components of a scientific argument, the rest of the paragraph is likely to have little meaning for you.

Frequent self-monitoring for understanding can be a powerful aid to improving your study efficiency in math and science courses. There is no general rule of thumb as to how often you should stop and check your understanding. It'll be up to you to stop and re-read whenever you find you didn't really understand something.

• **Brief same-day reviews are especially important.** Because of the sequential nature of math and science courses, brief same-day reviews will pay big dividends. Refreshing your memory of earlier information and steps will improve your understanding of current material.

• **Don't skip sections which are difficult to understand.** When reading a math or science textbook, there is a strong temptation to skip over equations and paragraphs you don't understand. Because the ideas in these texts follow a logical progression, each new idea builds on prior ideas. You'll soon become hopelessly lost if you skip things you don't understand.

• **When you read something you don't understand, go back rather than ahead.** In most cases, the reason you find material difficult is that the passage assumes you have prior knowledge. Skipping over the section and moving ahead won't give you this essential knowledge. It's usually a much better strategy to go back and relearn the earlier concepts you need to understand the present section.

• **Get help if you need it.** Rather than spending hours being hopelessly bogged down with something you can't understand, get help. If you've given it an honest try and still can't understand the reasoning, there's nothing wrong with asking for help. Talk to another student to see if they can help. Even better, ask your instructor to help explain the material. If your school has a tutorial service, keep this source of help in mind. Don't be afraid to ask for help when you need it!

☞ go to 3

3

## Problem-Solving Strategies

A major component in most mathematics and science courses is the ability to apply what you have learned in solving problems. Your ability to correctly solve problems in these courses will make a major contribution to your grades. To better understand the process of problem solving, let's examine what good problem solvers do.

Studies have found that students who are above average problem solvers tend to go through a series of systematic steps when they tackle a problem. Four steps are usually involved:

1. Use questions to state the problem.
2. Analyse the problem situation.
3. Look for possible solutions.
4. Test and verify solutions.

**Asking questions to state the problem**
This first stage of the problem-solving process involves asking questions to better understand the nature of the problem. Rephrase the problem in the form of a question. What is it you are trying to find out? What do you want to know? What difficulties are present? Use the question words what, how come, and why to help you ask questions to state the nature of the problem.

**Analyse the problem situation**
After you've stated the question in the problem, you should find out as much as you can about the problem. What do you know about it? What information do you need to solve the problem? What steps will be required to solve the problem? Where can you find more information? What will help you solve the problem? Are there similar problems elsewhere in the textbook or readings? What other sources of information could you use to solve the problem?

These or similar questions will help get you thinking of possible solutions and the information you'll need to come up with these solutions. During your analysis of the problem, you are really searching for more information. This stage forces you to obtain as much information as you can about a situation.

**Look for possible solutions**
After you've stated the question and analysed the problem, you're ready to start looking for possible solutions. At this stage it's important to resist the tendency to accept the first solution or answer that seems promising.

The real creativity of problem solving enters during this stage. Applying what you know, you come up with a solution. In the next stage, you'll check the accuracy of this solution.

**Test and verify solutions**
Once you've come up with a possible solution, the last step in problem solving is to test your answer to verify it. This is a step that is frequently overlooked by students. They work through until they've solved an equation and then move on to the next one without double-checking to see if their answer is correct. Although a few "kind-hearted" teachers will give you some credit for using the right process to solve a problem, you'll usually lose points if your answer is incorrect. The testing and verification stage of problem solving helps ensure the accuracy of your answers.

☞ go to 5

4

**Additional Tips for Problem Solving**
Problem solving in math and science courses will become easier if you give sufficient study to the material you need to know and adopt a systematic approach for tackling problems. Here are some additional tips which many students have found helpful:

• **Practice** With practice, problem solving becomes easier. Always do the practice exercises and assigned problems. Simply going through a sample solution in the text is seldom sufficient to allow you to readily solve a similar problem yourself. In a course which requires you to solve problems, don't spend all your study time just reading the text or rewriting your notes.

Although these activities are important, they are not the only focus of a problem-solving course.

• **Set a maximum attempt time.** Don't get bogged down on a single difficult problem. It's better to set a maximum time you will spend on any one problem (perhaps 20 to 30 minutes). At the end of this time, if you still haven't solved the problem, go on to something else or go back and review the material you need to solve the problem. (A neat thing about problem solving is that sometimes after a period of rest, a solution presents itself.) If that solution never appears, get help.

• **Use sketches to help solve math problems.** Making a sketch of the problem can be a good way to simplify the problem-solving process. Consider this problem, for example: Is it a better buy to purchase 2 pens for 79¢ or 3 pens for \$1.29? Your sketch of this simple problem might look like this:

 = 0.79

 = \$1.29

The sketch immediately tells you that you'll have to find the price of each pen in the sketch to determine the better buy. In the first case, you'll have to divide 0.79 by 2. The price of each pen in this example is thus 39.5 ¢. In the second case the price of each pen is 43 ¢. (Buy two pens rather than three!)

• **Try using different methods to solve the problem.** There are usually a number of different ways to solve most problems. Sometimes we become fixated on one way (which happens to be incorrect) and don't even think about trying new solutions.

• **Think about similar problems.** If you've already learned how to solve similar problems, think about how you solved them. A similar approach may work for the current problem. Perhaps the pattern for solving the earlier problem will help you spot the cause of troubles with the current problem.

• **Take the time to go back and learn what you need to know.** If you're having trouble with math problems because you've forgotten basic algebraic operations, go back and relearn this material. Don't feel badly about having to do this. We all forget technical information quite rapidly unless we continue to use it.

• **Try to predict the final answer.** Before you start trying to solve a problem ask yourself these questions: "What is the likely shape of the final answer?"; "How big is the final answer likely to be?" "What units of measurement will the final answer be in?" Even if you have to guess, make a prediction about what the final answer will look like. Your prediction will help give you a rough idea of what to expect for an answer.

• **List the data in a table before starting.** Don't bother with this when solving very simple problems. However, listing the data in a neat table can help when trying more difficult problems. Many students find that just rearranging the information into a table helps get them started on the way to a solution. Another benefit of a table is that it may show relationships in the data you didn't see before. It may also help you simplify the problem or see the steps required for the solution.

• **Record intermediate steps when using a calculator.** If you use a calculator for math problems (and who doesn't?), become a fanatic for recording each step of the solution. Writing down each of the intermediate calculations gives you a record to check if something goes wrong. Without this written record you pretty much have to go back to step one and start over again if your answer is wrong.

• **Attack easy parts first when you're stuck.** Some students wait for everything to "click into place" before they tackle a difficult problem. Unfortunately, this master plan may never appear. When you're stuck on a problem, try to just solve a part of the problem. Doing the preliminary work can help you get over the block.

• **Try working the problem using smaller numbers.** When trying to solve a problem with large and complex quantities, try first solving the problem using smaller numbers. (Use any smaller numbers except 1 and 0 — they have special computational characteristics.) Once you've solved the problem using smaller numbers, you've established a pattern. When you go back to the original question you'll have a pattern to follow.

• **Assign numbers to problems that don't have numbers.** This may be especially helpful in solving geometry problems. Geometrical relationships may be easier to see when you assign small numerical values to replace the more common letter designations in geometry.

• **Play with the numbers.** When all else fails, some students find it helpful to "play" with the numbers. Use a piece of scratch paper and write down whatever you think of. Perhaps you could try to factor the numbers. Maybe one number could be evenly divided by another number. This "playing" with the numbers may turn out to be of not much value. Then again, it just might suggest a relationship or pattern you previously missed. Many students report that this activity helps them come up with useful problem-solving ideas.

• **Check your answer against the criteria.** Once you've arrived at an answer, don't forget to check it. Check it against your original prediction of what the answer would look like. Check to make sure that the answer looks reasonable. Does your answer meet the requirements of the problem? Are you sure you didn't make any computational errors in reaching the answer?

• **Check for your most common mistakes.** When you're checking for computational accuracy, keep an eye open for the types of mistakes you've made in the past. Do you tend to misplace decimal places? Do you sometimes forget to square numbers? Do you sometimes mess up the correct order of operations? You know what mistakes you've made in prior problems. Recheck your current calculations to see that you haven't repeated them again.

• **Give it a rest.** If you're really at a dead-end, give it a rest. Put down the problem. Take a break and do something else. Part of your mind will keep working on the problem during your break. (Psychologists call this "incubation.") When you come back to the problem a solution may present itself.

• **When you're really stuck, seek alternate help.** Use your textbook and notes first. If this doesn't help, ask your teacher's help. Don't be afraid to ask for help. Requesting help is a sign of a student who wants to learn. Teachers respect this kind of motivation and are pleased to help you understand.

☞ go to **6**

**5**

This section contains an example of how you might use the four steps of the problem-solving process to attack a math problem. Suppose that you are taking Mathematics 300 and find yourself facing a page of linear equations in three unknowns which you must solve.

At this point, you've probably read how to use various methods to solve such equations and may have gone through a practice solution given in the textbook. You take a deep breath and tackle the first set of equations. They look like this:

| | |
|---|---|
| (Equation 1) | $2x - 3y + 5z = 27$ |
| (Equation 2) | $x + 2y - z = -4$ |
| (Equation 3) | $5x - y + 4z = 27$ |

Let's apply the four stage model of problem solving to arriving at the solution. Recall that the four steps are:

*1.* use questions to state the problem
*2.* analyse the problem situation
*3.* look for possible solutions
*4.* test and verify solutions.

*Step 1: Ask questions to state the problem.*

You should start by looking at the directions to see exactly what you are supposed to do in the problem. After you've had a look, you see that you are being asked to solve this set of linear equations each containing three unknowns.

Your next question might be "How am I supposed to solve the equations?" Looking further, you see that the directions specify that you use the method of elimination to derive your solution.

Next, you might ask yourself what form your final answers will take. Again you see that there are three unknowns in the equations. The problem thus requires a solution which provides values for each of the three unknowns.

You now have enough information about the problem to proceed to the next step. You know what the problem is, what method you must use to arrive at the solution, and that your solution will provide values for three different unknowns.

*Step 2: Analyse the problem situation.*

At this point in solving the equations you should ask yourself what you know about using the method of elimination. Have you read the appropriate section in the textbook? If not, return and study it.

Is there a practice example for using the method of elimination to solve linear equations? If so, make sure that you have worked through it.

Basically, the analysis step gives you a chance to see what you know and how this knowledge might be applied to the problem. You are "gathering" all of your knowledge in preparation for applying it to solving those three equations.

*Step 3: Looking for possible solutions (and applying them).*

The prior step gave you an idea of what you'll need to know to solve the equations. Now you're ready to apply this knowledge in looking for possible solutions. The process might look something like this:

You remember that the text example told you to find two equations and eliminate one unknown in both these equations. Following this step, you decide to try eliminating the unknown z between equations 1 and 2.

If you've learned previous lessons, you'll know how to eliminate the unknown z. In this case, you can eliminate the unknown z by multiplying equation 2 by 5. Your first step in solving the equations then looks like this:

| | |
|---|---|
| (Equation 1) | $2x - 3y + 5z = 27$ |
| (Equation 2) x 5 | $5x + 10y - 5z = -20$ |

From prior lessons, you know that to get rid of the unknown z from each of these equations, all you have to do is add the two equations. Your computations look like this:

| | |
|---|---|
| (Equation 1) | $2x - 3y + 5z = 27$ |
| (Equation 2) x 5 | $5x + 10y - 5z = -20$ |
| (Equation 4) | $7x + 7y = 7$ |

At this point you're well on your way to a solution. You've eliminated the unknown z from equation 4. What next? From your analysis of what was required to solve the problem, you now remember that the next step is to proceed and also eliminate the z between equations 2 and 3. You know that you can do this by following the same approach you used with equations 1 and 2. In this case, you can eliminate the z from equations 2 and 3 by multiplying equation 2 by 4. Your computations look like this:

| | |
|---|---|
| (Equation 2) x 4 | $4x + 8y - 4z = -16$ |
| (Equation 3) | $5x - y + 4z = 27$ |
| (Equation 5) | $9x + 7y = 11$ |

You're feeling pretty good at this point because now you realize that you've got two equations (Equations 4 and 5) which each contain only two unknowns. Because you've mastered an earlier lesson on how to solve such equations, you know that you can solve these two equations by simple subtraction. Your computation for this stage looks like this:

| | |
|---|---|
| (Equation 4) | $7x + 7y = 7$ |
| (Equation 5) | $9x + 7y = 11$ |
| Subtraction: | $-2x = -4$ |

So, $x = 2$

Substituting $x = 2$ in equation 4 gives you:

$$7(2) + 7y = 7$$
$$7y = -7$$

So, $y = -1$

Bingo! You've now got a value for x and a value for y. It's child's play to take these values and substitute them into equation 1 to find the value for z. Your computation looks like this:

(Equation 1) $2x - 3y + 5z = 27$

$$2(2) - 3(-1) + 5z = 27$$
$$5z = 27 - 4 - 3 = 20$$

So, $z = 4$

You've now come up with a tentative solution. Your calculations suggest that the value of $x = 2$, that $y = -1$, and that $z = 4$. Time to move to the next stage of the problem-solving process.

*Stage 4: Testing and verifying solutions.*

Checking the accuracy of your answers in this problem is a simple matter. Just plug your obtained values into the appropriate places in each of the three original equations and see if your values produce an equality. Your verification looks like this:

(Equation 1)

$$2x - 3y + 5z = 27$$
$$2(2) - 3(-1) + 5(4) = 27$$
$$4 + 3 + 20 = 27$$
$$27 = 27$$

(Equation 2)

$$x + 2y - z = -4$$
$$1(2) + 2(-1) - 1(4) = -4$$
$$2 - 2 - 4 = -4$$
$$-4 = -4$$

(Equation 3)

$$5x - y + 4z = 27$$
$$5(2) - (-1) + 4(4) = 27$$
$$10 + 1 + 16 = 27$$
$$27 = 27$$

Things are looking good. You've applied a solution, come up with three potential answers for the unknown values, and checked your answers. Even better, your answers checked out! Naturally, if they didn't you should go back to the drawing boards, find out where you went wrong, and correct your solution.

☞ go to **4**

**6**

None of the learning strategies in this chapter will do you much good if you don't get into the habit of using them. You are obviously interested in improving your learning efficiency in math and science courses or you wouldn't have bothered with this chapter. Resolve to carry through on your good intentions by selecting and using the tips in this chapter which seem most useful to you.

Briefly review the various survival strategies included in this chapter. Then use the following space to record the strategies which you plan to use.

I plan to use the following survival strategies to improve my study efficiency in math and science courses:

-------------------------------------------------
-------------------------------------------------
-------------------------------------------------
-------------------------------------------------
-------------------------------------------------
-------------------------------------------------
-------------------------------------------------
-------------------------------------------------
-------------------------------------------------
-------------------------------------------------
-------------------------------------------------
-------------------------------------------------
-------------------------------------------------
-------------------------------------------------
-------------------------------------------------
-------------------------------------------------
-------------------------------------------------
-------------------------------------------------
-------------------------------------------------
-------------------------------------------------

Periodically return to this page to remind yourself of your new learning plans. Give yourself a well deserved pat on the back if you've been successful in using your new learning strategies. If you've gradually stopped using the strategies, freshen your resolve and give it another try. They've worked for other students and you can put them to work for yourself.

When you're ready to continue on in the workbook, go to another chapter that looks most useful.

"OH, DEAR! ANOTHER TRAGIC CASE OF MATH ANXIETY!"

# CHAPTER 7
# Improving Performance on Tests

**In this chapter you can learn**

- *how to prepare for an examination*
- *how to become more "test-wise"*
- *how to be less anxious about examinations*

Examinations are a regular part of school work and learning to do better on tests will raise your grades. This chapter will help remove some of the trial-and-error from taking tests. Like any skill, you can learn strategies to improve your performance on examinations.

There are three ways to improve how well you do on tests. The most important is to increase your mastery of the material. You can also improve your test performance by learning how to take tests more intelligently. Lastly, if you become highly anxious about tests, you will do better once you learn to reduce your test anxiety.

To see if you might benefit from some of these test-taking strategies, please answer this checklist.

| Yes | No | |
|---|---|---|
| ☐ | ☐ | 1. I am usually well prepared for tests. |
| ☐ | ☐ | 2. I usually spend several days before a test reviewing material not just learning it for the first time. |
| ☐ | ☐ | 3. I eat and sleep normally the last few days before a big test. |
| ☐ | ☐ | 4. I make a point of knowing what topics will be covered on a test and study accordingly. |
| ☐ | ☐ | 5. I use tests from prior years to learn more about a teacher's testing style. |
| ☐ | ☐ | 6. When a test is approaching, I plan ahead and schedule study and review time for the test. |
| ☐ | ☐ | 7. Before a test, I quiz myself. |
| ☐ | ☐ | 8. Before a test, I participate in a study group for review. |

Congratulations if you answered "Yes" to each of these items. By engaging in each of these activities you are doing a good job of preparing for tests. If you are interested in seeing if there are ways you could become even better prepared for tests, go to section **1**. Otherwise...

☞ go to **2**

Answering "No" to one or more of these items indicates that you can probably improve your school grades by applying new ways of preparing for examinations. The strategies of section **1** will be helpful.

☞ go to **1**

**1**

## Preparing for Exams

Naturally, how well you do on an examination will be related to how well you have learned the material. Research shows that those students who do well on tests have at least one thing in common. Their preparation for examinations starts on the first day of class and continues until they write the exam.

How well you prepare for an exam will determine how well you do on that exam. You may wonder why we're repeating such an "obvious" conclusion. The reason is straightforward. There are a surprising number of students who show very poor preparation for exams and yet are shocked when their test performance matches their level of preparation.

All of the strategies in earlier chapters can help you be better prepared for examinations. They are all proven ways to increase your mastery of what you study. Examinations are designed to measure this mastery. Improving your study efficiency will pay big dividends when examination day rolls around!

Start by joining the ranks of the best students. These are the ones, you'll remember, who start preparing for exams on the first day of classes. Use the strategies of earlier chapters to improve your level of preparation for examinations. To refresh your memory, some of these important strategies include:

1. Take good lecture notes. Distill the main points and identify key ideas. Review your notes shortly after class and periodically throughout the term.

2. Use SQ3R study strategies on all assigned readings.

3. Schedule periodic review. Review at various times during the school term. Don't wait until the last minute before the exam. Your retention of material will be much better if you space reviews rather than cramming them into the last day or so before the test.

4. Save the last few days before an examination for an intensive review. This is particularly important for "big" exams like finals.

By using these strategies you will naturally increase your mastery of coursework and it'll show come exam time. Remember that regular, active study together with spaced reviews produces the best learning. Exams are really nothing more than a way in which your teacher measures that learning.

So what else can you do to better prepare for exams? Actually there are a number of exam preparation tips which many students have found to be very useful. Some of these tips include:

• **Test yourself before the examination.** Your self-test is like a dress rehearsal for the examination. While there is still enough time to brush up material you don't know, give yourself a self-test. Better yet, form a study group with a friend or two. Use a group review period to quiz each other. One member of the group can use the textbook and notes as a source of questions to ask the others. Then change roles so everyone gets a chance to answer as well as ask questions. Self-tests and group study "testing" can be very helpful in monitoring how well you've really mastered the material. It's much better to find out what you don't know before the exam. That way you'll still have time for pre-examination mastery of the material.

• **Find out as much as you can about the exam.** Try to find the answers to questions like these: "What material will be on the exam?" "What is the relative importance of different topics on the exam?" "What type of test will it be (e.g. multiple-choice, essay, short answer, etc.)?" "What is the time limit for the exam?" Start by simply asking the instructor about the exam. Most instructors will tell you a great deal about the organization of an exam if you just ask.

• **Try to predict what might be stressed on the exam.** Use cues such as how much emphasis your teacher placed on topics in class to try to predict what might be on the exam. If your instructor spent a great deal of class time on a particular topic, you'll probably run into this topic again in the examination. Obviously, the safest strategy is to learn all of the assigned material. But it never hurts to pay extra attention to material the instructor obviously feels is important!

• **Learn the teacher's testing habits.** Like most of us, teachers tend to be creatures of habit. They tend to favour tests with the same general organization. It's helpful to prepare for an examination by looking at examinations from prior years from the same teacher. These tests will show you the teacher's preference for essay or multiple-choice items and the topics emphasized for testing. Some teachers are fanatics for details while others prefer to test on the "big picture." Looking at prior exams can help you predict and prepare for the types of questions likely to appear on the upcoming exam. Knowing what to expect and studying accordingly can help reduce the amount of time it takes to prepare for an exam.

• **During review, ask yourself questions you think might be on the test.** If you've used SQ3R and the notetaking tips from earlier chapters, you'll already know what the key points and major ideas are when you start reviewing for the exam. This knowledge, along with what you know about the organization of the test and the teachers testing habits, can help you ask yourself questions which are likely to be on the test. This is an important test preparation skill. With a little practice, don't be surprised if you end up being able to predict more than half of the questions which finally do actually appear on the test! If you've predicted and studied them beforehand, answering them on the test will be a snap!

• **Prepare for the type of test questions you expect.** If you expect multiple-choice questions on the exam pay attention to details as well as main concepts. Essay questions are more complicated. Besides having to recall the main details and supporting facts, they require that you be able to organize your answers. When studying for essay tests, it's a good idea to make a short outline for how you will answer likely essay questions. Your outline will provide a framework for organizing your thoughts during the exam.

• **Maintain a healthy lifestyle before the test.** In the final crunch, a good nights sleep before a test will probably do you more good than a few hours of extra study. It's also a good idea to start the day with a decent breakfast. That way you'll come to the examination rested and well nourished. Your mind will work better if you have taken good care of your body.

• **If you really must cram for the exam, do it intelligently!** The best advice is to plan regular study before exams so you don't have to cram. If cramming is your style, at the very least give yourself a break by allowing a few extra days for cramming. If the last day before the exam is usually "panic city," take some of the panic out of cramming by scheduling an extra day or two for your last minute learning. You'll be more relaxed if you give yourself more time and you'll end up learning more.

If procrastination gets the best of you and you find yourself in a real bind, try to cram more intelligently. Select very carefully how you will spend those precious few minutes of study time. Pick out only the most important parts of your notes or text for study. If (heaven forbid) you don't have time for a thorough reading of material which will be on the test, use a survey to get general information. Do the best you can with your time. Use your time to work on very carefully selected items. Before the next exam, have a look at some of the tips for avoiding procrastination in Chapter 3.

• **Be anti-social right before an exam.** It's generally a good idea to avoid talking with other nervous students right before a major exam. Test anxiety can be contagious!

☞ **go to 2**

**2**

The second part of this chapter investigates ways you can do better on examinations by becoming more "test-wise." To see if these test-taking strategies might be useful to you, please answer the following checklist.

| Yes | No | |
|---|---|---|
| ☐ | ☐ | 1. I know the key words that instructors use to describe what they want done on a test. |
| ☐ | ☐ | 2. At the start of a test, I plan how much time I will spend on each part of the test. |
| ☐ | ☐ | 3. I usually answer the easy test items first. |
| ☐ | ☐ | 4. When I don't know the answer to a test item, I usually make a guess. |
| ☐ | ☐ | 5. I know the "clue" words which often tell if a test statement is true or false. |
| ☐ | ☐ | 6. I know the "clue" words for essay questions which indicate what the teacher wants. |
| ☐ | ☐ | 7. I know a systematic approach which can help me do better on multiple-choice questions. |
| ☐ | ☐ | 8. I know a systematic approach which can help me do better on essay questions. |

If you answered "Yes" to all of these items, you may already know and use all of the test-taking strategies covered in section **3** . If you feel that you don't need improvement in your test-taking skills...

☞ **go to 4**

If you answered "No" to some of the above items, you will find the test-taking strategies of section **3** useful in improving your performance during examinations.

☞ **go to 3**

**3**

## Becoming "Test-Wise"

All of the strategies of this section fall in the category of working smarter, not harder. By helping you take tests more systematically and intelligently, they can help you do better by becoming "test-wise."

**Making it or breaking it in the first five minutes.** What you do during the first five minutes of a test is extremely important. You'll do much better on the test if you use this time wisely. Here are some of the most important things to do during the initial minutes of an exam:

• **Put your name on the test papers or answer sheets.** You'd be surprised how many students turn in test papers without their names. Do this little chore first. (It gets you off on the right foot because this is one "question" that you won't have any difficulty answering.)

• **Read and understand the general directions.** After your name appears everywhere it should, read the instructions or directions given with the test. Don't skip over the directions in an effort to save time. Listen carefully if the instructor gives any additional verbal instructions. It's a good idea to underline any key words in the directions.

When you're reading the test directions look for answers to questions like these: "Do I have to answer all of the questions or is there a choice?" (Notice the appearance of the words "and" and "or." i.e. "Answer three questions from Part A and three questions from Part B" versus "Answer three questions from Part B or three questions from Part B.") "How am I supposed to record my answers?" (e.g. on an answer sheet or directly on the test paper) "Can I write with either a pen or pencil or do I have to use a special pencil for computer scoring?" "Should answers go right on the examination or on a separate answer sheet or booklet?"

Be sure to read all of the directions in the test. General instructions appear at the beginning, but different parts of the test may also have directions. Be sure to also read these instructions if present. See Box 8 for a summary of key words which frequently appear in examination directions.

Box 8

**Key Terms and What They Ask You To Do**

Here are some key terms which frequently appear in test directions along with what the teacher expects you to do.

| | |
|---|---|
| **Analyse** | Identify the components of something and examine these elements. |
| **State** | Describe something. Usually a brief description is all that is required. You won't have to elaborate your answer. |
| **Describe** | Give a written account of the characteristics of the subject. |
| **Discuss** | Tell what you know about the topic. Include those things which are relevant to the question. |
| **List** | Very briefly present all of the parts or elements which form the whole. Extensive discussions are not required. Simply list the key parts. |
| **Trace** | Describe in words how something developed. Identify what led from the origin to the present conclusion. |
| **Outline** | Using a very concise form, list the main points or ideas. Elaborate descriptions are not required. |
| **Summarize** | Identify and briefly describe the main points. |
| **Diagram** | Make an outline of the chief features of the topic using a diagram. Be sure to clearly label all important features of your diagram. |
| **Define** | Give the definition. Clearly specify the unique characteristics and qualities of what you are defining. |
| **Prove )**<br>**Show that )**<br>**Justify )** | Demonstrate the validity of something by presenting arguments or evidence. |
| **Illustrate** | Use charts, diagrams, or specific examples to explain something. |
| **Explain** | Use simpler more explicit terms to state the subject. |
| **Demonstrate** | Use examples to prove the point. |
| **Compare** | Describe the similarities and differences of two or more things. |
| **Contrast** | Describe the differences between two or more things. |
| **Relate** | Describe the connection between two or more things. |
| **Evaluate** | Judge the subject. Is it true and accurate? Is it significant? Is it worthwhile? Is it pleasing or beautiful? |

(Adapted from: Grassick, P. (1983) *Making the grade: How to score high on all scholastic tests* New York: Arco)

If you don't understand any of the directions, don't be afraid to ask the test administrator for clarification.

**Survey the entire test.**
At this point you've put your name on the test and you understand the directions. It's time now to spend a few minutes making a survey of the test contents. Notice how many questions are on the exam and how many pages it has. Make sure that there are no pages missing. Do you have any choice of questions to answer in different sections? "Which questions look easiest?"

If short-answer or essay questions appear on the test, take a minute during your survey to quickly read these questions. Also notice how much weight is assigned to different sections of the test. If one section is worth more points than other sections, you'll know that you should spend your time accordingly.

**Jot down initial thoughts.**
During your initial survey of the test, jot down any thoughts you have about specific questions. A word or two by each question will help remind you of key points concerning your answer. If you write down these initial ideas during your survey, you won't have to struggle to remember them later when you're answering the question.

**Plan how you will spend your time during the exam.**
Portion out your time according to the worth of different exam sections. For example, if you have an hour for the exam and 50% of the grade is given to short answer or essay questions and 50% of the grade is given to multiple-choice questions, allot 30 minutes to the objective questions and 30 minutes to the written answer questions. Keep an eye on the time during an exam to make sure that you aren't spending too much time on one part of the exam. Don't give more work to an item than it is worth.

When planning your time, remember to allow a few minutes at the end to review your answers.

## Tips for Answering Test Items

If you follow the above strategies, a few minutes into the test you already know a number of things about it. You have an idea of what is expected. You've surveyed the test. You know what types of questions it contains and their value. You've also planned how you will use your time. You're ready now to start answering the test questions. Here are some tips which can help you tackle those questions with better results:

• **Remember to read directions carefully.** I've said it twice because it's important. Make sure you know what is expected before you start answering. In nearly every set of examinations I've ever marked, I've seen some very excellent answers to the wrong question It would be worth your while to carefully review the meaning of the common examination terms presented in Box 8.

• **Start with the easy questions.** On a multiple choice exam, start with the first question and try to answer it. Go on until you run into difficulty or can't answer a question. Skip that question for the time being and go on to another. By initially doing only those items you can answer, you get yourself going and build momentum. Answering the easy items first will also help give you a sense of accomplishment. Make sure to mark those items you don't answer so you can come back and work on them later.

On short answer or essay items it's less important to try and answer the items in the order in which they appear. Look through all of the essay questions and start first with the one you find easiest. Then go on to a more difficult question. While you are writing your answer to the easy item, you will be remembering ideas for the more difficult questions.

• **Try to think of the correct answer before looking at multiple choice options.** On multiple choice questions, try to think of the correct answer as soon as you've read the question. Do this even before you look at each of the possible response options. If you can readily remember the answer to the question, it will help you rapidly eliminate incorrect response options.

• **Spot key words in objective test questions.** True and false questions, multiple choice questions, completion or fill-in items, and matching questions are all examples of objective test questions. These questions are called "objective" because they have a correct answer. Scoring objective items is a purely mechanical process which can be done by a machine.

Research shows that the most common reason students fail objective tests is not lack of knowledge. Instead, the students ability to reason with what they know is more important. When you are taking an objective test, it is very important therefore that you be able to read and interpret the objective questions correctly.

Let's do a little reasoning about dealing with objective test items. Suppose that you are faced with a series of True-False items on an exam. Because they are objective items, they were designed by your teacher so that each item would be absolutely true or absolutely false. Suppose that your teacher asks this question:

"Children of alcoholics become alcoholics themselves. (True or false?)"

The teacher cannot grade this question. When you study the literature on alcoholism you find that this question is sometimes true and sometimes false. Other factors are also involved which are not specified in the question. Instead of phrasing the question this way, your teacher would be more likely to offer one of the following versions:

"Children of alcoholics *always* become alcoholics themselves."

"Children of alcoholics *never* become alcoholics themselves."

"Children of alcoholics *sometimes* become alcoholics themselves."

The first two questions are obviously false and the last question is true. The words in these questions which offer clues as to the truth or falsity of the item are always, never, and sometimes. They take a sweeping generalization and trim it down to size. See Box 9 for a more complete list of clue words that frequently appear in objective test items.

Box 9

**Clue Words in Objective Test Items**

These clue words can be a big help in deciding whether a statement in an objective test item is true or false.

| *Group 1* | *Group 2* | *Group 3* | *Group 4* |
|---|---|---|---|
| **Every** | **Often** | **More** | **Best** |
| **All** | **Usually** | **Equal** | **Good** |
| **Always** | **Sometimes** | **Less** | **Bad** |
| **Only** | **Seldom** | **Most** | **Worst** |
| **Never** | **Rarely** | **Some** | |
| **None** | **Occasionally** | **Few** | |
| **Without exception** | **Frequently** | **Several** | |
| **Necessarily** | **Approximately** | **Many** | |
| **Invariably** | | | |

*Group 1 Clue Words*: When these words appear in an objective test item, they indicate that the statement is absolutely true. Can you think of any exceptions to the statement? If you can think of an exception, then the statement is false. (With the possible exception of science, mathematics, and in definitions, statements containing Group 1 clue words are often false.)

*Group 2 Clue Words*: When these words appear in an objective test item, they require that you make a judgment of the frequency or probability with which something occurs. Statements containing these words should receive very careful consideration because they could very well be true. When answering objective items containing these clue words, try to remember information and facts which will help you decide if the indicated frequency of occurrence is true or false.

*Group 3 Clue Words*: These clue words state magnitudes. When you see these clue words, try to remember facts and information about the sizes of relationships, how often something occurred, etc. Use this information to help you decide if the stated magnitude is consistent with what you remember reading about it.

*Group 4 Clue Words*: Group 4 clue words imply a judgment. The clue words "best" and "worst" are easiest. If you can think of an exception, then the statement is false.

• **Treat multiple choice items like True-False items.** In a multiple choice item, each response option really becomes a true-false item. That response, when combined with the stem of the question, makes the statement true or false. Look for the clue words of Box 9 in each multiple choice response option and use them to help you decide if that option is true or false. When you decide that an option is false, draw a line through it to indicate that you have eliminated that option.

• **Check grammatical consistency in multiple choice questions.** Some teachers are not careful in matching the grammar of multiple choice items so that it is consistent with the grammar of the question stem. For example, in a multiple choice question, the correct answer will usually agree in gender, number, and person with the stem of the question. If a response option disagrees with the grammar of the stem, it's probably not the answer. Here's an example:

> SQ3R is a
> a) activity for improving physical strength.
> b) method for learning more efficiently.
> c) evil robot from an Isaac Asimov novel.
> d) integrated approach to speed reading.

Option b is the only one which is consistent grammatically with the question stem. All of the other options require the article "an" rather than "a" in the stem.

• **Answer every question.** It's a good idea to answer every objective item on a test, even if the test will be graded for a penalty for guessing. On most objective exams, your score will be the number of correct answers minus the number of incorrect answers. Even if you don't have a clue as to which of four response options is correct, you can usually eliminate at least one of the options as incorrect. Your chances of being correct on that item are at least 25% and perhaps higher if you can eliminate one or more of the incorrect options. Clearly, you aren't being "test wise" if you fail to answer all objective items.

• **Change answers or leave them alone?** When marking objective tests, it's always interesting to look at answers that have been changed. My own informal tally suggests that it is more common to find that the initial answer was correct. In some cases, however, students do improve their score by reconsidering and changing early answers. So what should you do?

It's probably a good idea to use your own individual test taking style as a guide. Are you the type of student who is very anxious during the first part of an exam but who settles down once you get into the swing of it? Or are you the type of student whose anxiety level increases at the end of the exam as you realize that you are running out of time? If you're more anxious at the beginning of an exam, it might improve your score if you review your early work very closely and make necessary changes. On the other hand, if you get nervous as you are running out of time, don't even consider making last minute changes to your earlier work.

• **Jot down initial ideas for an essay question next to the question.** A good way to start organizing your thoughts for an essay question is to simply write down any initial ideas next to the question. As you think more about the question, expand on these points. Don't worry yet whether the ideas are good or how you will organize them. Just write them down so you don't forget them.

• **Number your points and ideas.** When you think you have enough points to answer the question, start organizing your answer by numbering the ideas and points in the order in which they'll be used. At this point you can do some editing. Discard those ideas that are not relevant. Use this numbered list of points to get started writing your answer.

• **Leave extra space in answers to essay questions.** It's a good idea to leave a space at the end of your answer before beginning the next answer. That way, if other ideas come to mind later, you'll have a place to add them. Also leave some space at the top of the page. Use this space if you want to rewrite or add something

• **Have an emergency plan for finishing essays when you run out of time.** This paragraph could be subtitled "How to fight off panic when you notice you have only 3 minutes to finish the last essay question." On occasion, you may misjudge your time allocation and end up with more questions than time to answer them. In these emergency situations, try to write an expanded outline for an answer to an essay question rather than trying to complete a full answer.

• **Check grammar and spelling.** Reserve a few minutes to re-read your essay answers. If time allows, make necessary corrections to grammar and spelling. If more examples would strengthen your answers, add them. Is your handwriting legible? If not, rewrite or print any sections which resemble chicken scratching.

• **Check to see that you have answered all questions.** Before leaving the exam, double check to see that you haven't missed any questions. I've had students who have left an exam early only to discover to their horror that they overlooked an entire page of questions!

• **Ignore what other students do during the test.** If some students start leaving the examination room before the end of the available time, don't feel rushed. Take all the time you need. Work at your own pace. In fact, it's probably a good idea to never leave an exam until you have to. If you finish early, use the rest of the time to review your answers, improve subjective answers, check the accuracy of your work, etc. Don't leave the exam until they throw you out!

• **Don't forget to use every test as a learning experience.** When tests are returned, most students do little except moan about the grade. You can become more "test-wise" if you treat a returned test as a potential learning experience. It offers you to discover your mistakes so that you don't make them again on the next test.

What should you look for? First look to see if the instructor has added any comments to the exam. These comments will often point out deficiencies in your answers or why you lost points on a particular item. It's a good idea to compare your answers with those from other students who did better on the exam. Why did you lose points? Did you misinterpret the meaning of the question? Did you forget some important details or ideas? Was your answer poorly organized? By analysing your mistakes in this fashion you can prevent the same thing from happening on the next exam.

☞ go to **4**

**4**

Are you tense and anxious during examinations? To see if you could benefit from learning how to manage test anxiety, please answer the following checklist.

| Yes | No | |
|---|---|---|
| ❑ | ❑ | 1. I would do better if I wasn't so anxious during examinations. |
| ❑ | ❑ | 2. I sometimes feel a sense of panic before or during an exam. |
| ❑ | ❑ | 3. I often "know" an answer but can't remember it during a test. |

If you answered "No" to each of these items, there is no need to read the section on managing test anxiety.

☞ go to **6**

If you answered "Yes" to some of these items, you can benefit from strategies for managing test anxiety.

☞ go to **5**

**5**

## Managing Test Anxiety

Many students experience some anxiety before and during tests. This is natural and is quite normal. After all, exams are just a little threatening. At exam time the moment of truth has arrived. How well you do on exams will make the difference between passing and failing or between a good grade versus a mediocre one.

Although some anxiety about exams is normal (and is even desirable), some students become so anxious about exams that their performance on tests is seriously affected. I can recall an extreme example from my own days as a graduate student. At the end of our first two years in the graduate program, all of the psychology graduate students had to write a series of "preliminary qualifying" examinations. This week long series of examinations tested everything we had learned in our graduate studies. Performance on the exams was the key factor that determined if we would be admitted to doctoral studies, and all of us knew that in previous years many students had failed and were asked to leave graduate school.

Needless, to say we all took those examinations very seriously and they generated a great deal of anxiety. Several students, however, buckled under the pressure and actually experienced breakdowns during prelim week.

Fortunately, most exams don't generate this much pressure. But that doesn't mean that your anxiety level during tests isn't affecting how well you do. Research shows that a moderate level of anxiety actually improves your performance on tests. It gives you the energy and motivation to prepare well for the test and to focus your effort during the exam. High levels of anxiety have the opposite effect. They make concentration difficult and can impair your ability to remember what you have studied. If you experience moderate or high levels of anxiety before or during exams, you can benefit from strategies to reduce test anxiety.

Three strategies for controlling test anxiety are presented in the following paragraphs. These approaches have been found useful by students with mild to moderate levels of test anxiety.

If test anxiety is a severe problem for you, it would be advisable to seek additional help from a teacher or counsellor at your school. Many learning centres at colleges run special programs to help students reduce test anxiety. Check to see if such a program or other assistance is available at your school.

**Three Strategies for Controlling Test Anxiety**

Three easy-to-apply strategies for managing test anxiety are:
**overpreparation**
**deep breathing**
**positive cognitions**

• **Controlling test anxiety with overpreparation.** Examinations are stressful because they place demands upon students. They demand that you show that you've learned and mastered the material. In any stressful situation, stress can be reduced whenever you are able to exercise more control over the source of the stress. It follows from this short discussion that one important way of reducing the stress associated with tests is to exercise more control over understanding and mastering the material being tested. Most students can readily think of personal examples where their own test anxiety varied in relation to how well they studied for a test. Chances are you were less anxious when you were well prepared for a test.

In a very real way, all of the learning strategies of prior chapters represent ways of reducing test anxiety. If used in a systematic plan of study, they will increase your mastery and retention giving you much less to be anxious about in tests. SQ3R, for example, is actually designed to produce overpreparation. This type of overlearning allows you to enter an examination knowing that you have mastered the material. Naturally you'll feel less anxious under these conditions.

In summary, one important way of reducing test anxiety is to plan your pre-test studies so that you have a good mastery and understanding of assigned material. Not only does overpreparation reduce test anxiety, it can also give you an entirely different feeling about exams. Instead of dreading exams, a well-prepared student anticipates them. For these students, exams represent an opportunity for showing their learning accomplishments.

• **Relaxing with Deep Breathing.** A good way of handling temporary feelings of anxiety is to relax with deep breathing. When you become anxious, you tend to take shallow and short breaths. This breathing pattern is easily broken by taking a series of deep and slow breaths. It's simple. All you have to do is to take in a deep breath, hold it for a few seconds, and then slowly release the breath. It may help to also imagine tension and anxiety leaving your body with the breath as you exhale. Wait a few minutes and repeat the deep breathing process again.

This deep breathing exercise is actually very similar to the type of breathing taught in the Lamaze method of natural childbirth. Besides being relaxing, it helps control pain.

Taking several slow, deep breaths can be very effective when you are feeling anxiety or panic. Monitor your own periods of high test anxiety and apply deep breathing at these times. If you're most anxious as you try to go to sleep the night before a big exam, use the deep breathing exercise. Try deep breathing if you feel yourself tensing up as you head for the test room. Perhaps you feel a mounting sense of panic as tests are being distributed or when you notice that you are running out of time. Try using the deep breathing relaxation procedure during these times.

• **Using positive cognitions to reduce test anxiety.** A great deal of test anxiety is caused by worries. You worry when you think about all of the terrible things that might happen. The next time you find yourself feeling test anxiety, monitor your thoughts. What were you thinking? Were you thinking about never being able to remember everything you've studied? Were you thinking about your parents' reactions if you do badly on the test? Perhaps you were thinking about how nervous you are. Maybe you were thinking about doing poorly on the last test and expecting the same thing to happen this time. You see the point. All of these negative thoughts nourish worry and anxiety.

Studies have shown that you can break out of this "worry pattern" by training yourself to think positively rather than negatively. When you give yourself positive messages in your thinking, you end up feeling better and worrying less.

This "positive thinking" is a proven way to increase your performance. It can even enhance physical performance. An important part of the sport psychology training used for Olympic athletes involves this type of positive thinking. Athletes are trained to think of themselves as winning and to visualize themselves breaking records. These "positive thoughts" have been shown to encourage athletes to give their best. They can do the same for students.

Apply this principle to controlling your own test anxiety and eliciting a personal peak performance during exams. When you notice yourself feeling uncomfortable levels of test anxiety, or thinking things which increase your tension, practice saying positive things to yourself. Instead of fretting, tell yourself that you know the material and you'll do fine. Remind yourself how intelligent you are. Think of prior good performances on tests. Come up with your own "positive self statements" which will get you thinking "success" rather than "failure." Some additional examples of positive self-thoughts which might be helpful are:

I can do it.

Don't worry, I really do know this stuff.

I'm going to do really well on this exam.

With the study I've put in, this is a piece of cake!

The last test was as hard as this and I did okay on that one.

I'll remember as soon as I relax a little.

Try using these or your own positive cognitions the next time you are feeling uncomfortably anxious about a test. They'll help get you in the same "mind set" as medal winning athletes.

☞ go to 6

**6**

This is the last section of the workbook. I hope you've enjoyed learning new strategies for studying smarter, not harder. Better yet, I hope that you've already started applying some of these strategies to your own coursework. It's worth the effort! Best wishes for becoming a more efficient lifelong learner.

# Notes